EMPOWERMENT COURSE HANDBOOK

HELEN HAMILTON

BALBOA.PRESS

A DIVISION OF HAY HOUSE

Balboa Press books may be ordered through booksellers or by contacting:

Balboa Press
A Division of Hay House
1663 Liberty Drive
Bloomington, IN 47403
www.balboapress.co.uk
UK TFN: 0800 0148647 (Toll Free inside the UK)
UK Local: 02036 956325 (+44 20 3695 6325 from outside the UK)

Print information available on the last page.

ISBN: 978-1-9822-8363-6 (sc)
ISBN: 978-1-9822-8364-3 (e)

Balboa Press rev. date: 06/08/2021

TABLE OF CONTENTS

Dedication

This work is dedicated to expounding the knowledge
necessary for consciousness to evolve and advance. It
is designed to allow peace and the end of suffering.
May all beings live a life of truth, love and peace.

CHAPTER I

Introduction

How to use this handbook

This handbook can be used on its own as a study guide to allow you to study the Empowerment courses by yourself. It can also be used to supplement the live courses with Helen. Whichever way you use it, this handbook contains all that is needed for you to be able to consciously create the life of your choosing through embracing all the information enclosed in here.

It is suggested that you spend time with each course in the order that they are presented here. Each lesson builds upon the previous one and each course adds to the previous one. You are urged to complete all three courses, even if you feel you do not need to focus on any particular one. For example, you may feel that you need help removing blocks to manifesting the abundance that you want but do not feel a pull to look at the Forgiveness Course. In such cases you are urged to pay particular attention to whatever you do not want to study, as this is usually resistance and avoidance from our mind. Even if we learn the technicalities of how to manifest what we want, we will be unable to allow it to happen for us if we still have self-hatred or unworthiness due to a lack of self-forgiveness.

All three courses are designed to work together to supply all the information your consciousness needs to know, to let go of all blocks and doubts. Only once you have read and digested each course will you have a complete set of tools to move forward.

The Empowerment Courses explained

These new courses are offered to supplement your own awakening process and to help you with the challenges that daily life can provide. These courses are ground-breaking as they offer vital information that every spiritual seeker needs to know to facilitate their own Self-Realisation in a simple way. Our consciousness needs certain information to be able to let go of resistance and move forward.

Most of our knowledge is based on worldly issues and challenges and we can all need some extra help to understand what we are, how we fit into the world and why we are here. These Empowerment Courses are designed to help you shift to a higher level of awareness, letting go of old blocks, resistances and karmic tendencies that are keeping you from living the life you deserve.

It is a belief that exists inside most of us that we already know what we need to know to evolve and expand our awareness and this is simply not true. Most of us need some extra information or a few myths cleared out of us, to allow ourselves to live a life of truth and advance our awakening. We are not automatically born with all of the information needed to live a life we desire and deserve. Many spiritual myths and false ideas have been absorbed by us over many lifetimes and these need to be exposed in order to move forward.

Let's now begin to study the courses one by one, beginning with the Forgiveness Course, followed by the Transcending the Vasanas Course and finishing with the Abundance, Manifestation and Desire Course.

This book contains all the course information that the students who participated in the live course received and all of the exercises that when completed thoroughly at each stage will allow you to move to a higher level of consciousness. It is important to do these exercises as they are designed to facilitate an absorption of the material and allow you to live from and as that knowledge. If you simply read the book and do not do the exercises, it will remain as only mental knowledge and you will not see the shifts happening in your life that you are looking for.

SECTION ONE

CHAPTER 2

The Forgiveness Course Introduction

Forgiveness is nothing to do with another person; it is all about you. In choosing this forgiveness course you have in effect chosen your own happiness, health and wellbeing. Numerous studies have been done on those that choose to forgive and the health benefits are scientifically proven and concrete. You will also experience greater peace, confidence and self-esteem as you learn the tools in this course. This is not to exclude the possibility that forgiving will make your outer life easier!

Forgiveness is a spiritual skill that can be easily learned and applied once you know how to do it and it will have deeply practical, everyday benefits. You can begin right now by forgiving yourself for the fact you could not forgive anyone consistently before now; you didn't have the tools, support or practice to do so. You wouldn't blame yourself for not being able to speak French fluently if you had not taken any lessons as yet! Forgiveness is a science which can be learned with the right information and time. Something that is difficult to forgive now can be forgiven effortlessly with the right skills.

It is important to know that forgiveness is not limited to a person who wronged you. Sometimes we can feel unconsciously angry, like towards a loved one that suddenly passed away and we may be holding onto a subtle blame that they should not have left us. We can also, for example, forgive the fact we never seem to have enough time or money.

Forgiveness can also be of ourselves. This is the most important part of our course because once we understand why we behave the way we have, we will find it easier to forgive others too. We will learn together that as human beings we are not supposed to be able to forgive easily right now, our brains are not wired that way. This doesn't mean that forgiving someone is only possible for a saint in a monastery or Mother Teresa; it simply means we cannot blame ourselves if we can't do it right now. We are usually much less forgiving of ourselves than others; we hold ourselves to a high, sometimes unreachable, standard simply due to the fact that we are human beings with real emotions and feelings.

Remember, most of humanity has no idea how, or the inclination to, learn to forgive. The fact that you are reading this means you are already an open-hearted person who wants the best for themselves and others.

CHAPTER 3

Forgiveness Course Lesson One
Forgiving Ourselves

What is forgiveness?

This subject may seem like a very basic question, yet over and over again, I find that people have a different idea of what forgiveness actually involves. It is vital that we start this course with a clear idea of what forgiving someone or ourselves actually means and you are encouraged to revisit this throughout the course.

Forgiving is really an acknowledgement of something that happened, will happen or might happen. It is acknowledging that something happened totally and not denying it happened at all. It is healing of our internal environment and a commitment to understand what it means to be human and the challenges that presents us with.

For-give-ness is a willingness to give away any feelings of "should" or "shouldn't" about a situation, person or ourselves. If we look at the root of the word "forgive" we see it is made of two parts; "for" and "give". "For" comes from a root word of "per" in Latin which means completely, absolutely or totally. "Give" means to let go of or release to someone or something else; to transfer to or remove from our possession.

We all have things we have "should" and "shouldn't" feelings about. Most of our opinions, judgements and attitudes would collapse completely if we suddenly let go of these "should" and "shouldn't" ideas. All conflict within ourselves would also stop and we would come to total peace immediately. The good news is that we do not have to let go of these; rather we simply have to acknowledge they are there. We are only asked to be honest that this is the way we feel. We can all do that right now. ☺

What forgiveness is not

- The ability to forgive is not some spiritual power that is earned as you reach higher levels of consciousness.
- It is not something that some people can simply do and somehow you missed out on it.
- Forgiveness is also not about publicly approaching anyone you may have negative feelings for or contacting them to say you forgive them.
- Forgiveness is not about feeling bliss and joy all the time.
- It is not mysterious or complicated.
- It is not something you are born with or not.

- Forgiveness is not a one-time event; we all can get better each day at forgiving ourselves and others if we want to. This is true no matter how advanced we may seem to others.
- And perhaps most importantly, forgiveness is not something you should know how to do already!

Forgiving ourselves

The first part of this course will be spent looking at forgiving ourselves first. This may seem unnecessary if you have joined this course to help you forgive someone that has wronged you; however I would urge you to fully engage in this lesson, as the benefits of this will unfold as we go along.

Why do we need to forgive ourselves?

As human beings, we all hold on to a thousand tiny self-inflicted wounds from times when we feel we have said the wrong thing in anger or made a wrong decision. We all have those moments of "it seemed like a good idea at the time" and lapses in judgement. Living in the world as a human being can be fun, exciting, dramatic, boring, difficult or even completely unfulfilling. We all have moments where we feel we should have coped better, should have remembered to ask friends for help, shouldn't have closed off and much more. Inside each of us is some energy of self-blame, guilt and there can even be self-loathing and hate for our perceived inadequacies as a person.

We are bombarded each day by media, adverts, social and peer pressure and familial expectations of what others expect our lives to be. Most of these expectations are highly unreasonable and often unreachable and yet we hold ourselves to blame silently inside each time we fail to live up to the expectations of others. Most of us also hold our own storehouse of self-expectations that are standards we hold ourselves to. Again, most of these are unrealistic and even based on fiction or untruth. We may watch a movie with friends and enjoy it but we are secretly comparing ourselves to the "good mother" from the movie and feeling inadequate. We may get ignored at work and passed over for promotion which can lead us to feel we are not doing a good enough job. Even when we excel at something, we can often feel that we need external recognition of our progress because our own inner judge is too quick to condemn us.

Other people's thoughts about us can often be unfounded opinions that are not based on any fact at all. We still somehow automatically take it on board when someone says something about us that is not nice. It is as if we have no filter sometimes between what goes in through our eyes and ears and what we believe to be true about ourselves. Because of all this our self-esteem can be badly damaged even if we seem to be a highly confident and successful person on the surface. On the contrary most of us try even harder to make up for what we perceive to be flaws in our character by putting in extra effort.

All of this can add up to make a noisy mind, low self-esteem and feeling like we can never quite measure up. We will start to heal this right now.

Why we cannot forgive

Reason 1 — We feel we should already be able to.

Most of us feel shame and guilt to some degree that we cannot forgive ourselves and we are stuck in a self-perpetuating loop. We cannot forgive that we cannot forgive as yet! This cycle goes around and around and guilt and shame build up in the depths of our psyche. We look at spiritual leaders of the past and present such as Gandhi, Mother Teresa and Christ and feel that somehow, we should be able to forgive the whole of humanity as they could. What we fail to acknowledge is that at some point they too went through this same process you are engaged in now. We feel stuck deep down in our progress because we cannot as yet admit where we are and acknowledge that is totally ok.

Admit that you are where you are and that is ok. There are things you like about yourself and things you do not like about yourself. There might always be things you don't like about yourself! Can you be ok with that? Yes you can. You are human and you are going to be experiencing and interacting with others for the rest of your life. It is unrealistic to expect that you will enjoy every encounter you have and leave it feeling enriched. You do not have to feel a connection with everyone you meet and most likely you will feel the opposite!

13

Somehow we have picked up a lie. That lie is that as human beings we should be equipped from birth to be able to forgive. That is simply not true.

Note this reason is especially valid if we are on a spiritual pathway or trying to better ourselves; which most of us are. We deeply believe that the more advanced we become spiritually, the more we should be able to let go and forgive effortlessly. This is simply not true! Forgiveness involves learning about yourself, how your thoughts and emotions work and the difference between left and right brain usage. If you have not had this information given to you as yet, then no matter how much you meditate or pray you simply will not be able to forgive - end of story!

It has been my experience that the more advanced we become spiritually the more life can ask of us also. We can be asked to forgive at a deeper level and in more challenging circumstances than we previously thought possible. For this reason alone, forgiveness may always be something we struggle with or feel challenged by. This is what it means to be human.

Reason 2 — We are scared to look at our feelings about ourselves and others.

Most of us have never been taught how to feel what we feel. There is no "Emotions 101" class at school and most adults we grow up with, also have no idea how to express emotions in a healthy way (through no fault of their own). As a result we learn to either suppress, project them onto others or vent our emotions and none of these is a healthy way to release emotions. We spend our lives pushing emotions down inside ourselves until we can feel like some sort of ticking time bomb that may go off at any second (and quite often does). When this happens we immediately blame ourselves and say that we should not do that. How can we blame ourselves for using a coping mechanism (albeit perhaps not the healthiest one) to survive?

We have come to believe that if we begin to look at what we have rejected within ourselves, it will have to be faced all at once and it will overwhelm us. This is not true and we can face it step-by-step. At any point you can take a break for an hour, a day or a year. Recognise that because you are reading this it means you are ready and able to look at this stack of emotions and begin to heal and release them.

It is not your fault you could not do this before. If you could have, you would have! Isn't it enough you are engaged in a course like this right now? What does that say about the kind of person you are?

Reason 3 — We haven't had the right information yet.

Nobody would expect you to be able to speak Spanish without taking Spanish lessons or spending a considerable amount of time in Spain. Somehow we know this is true but we expect ourselves to be able to forgive automatically.

Simply put, if nobody has shown you how to do it as yet then how can you be expected to know? If you have not received the correct information then your consciousness will not be able to assimilate it.

We will look at this more deeply in lesson two but for now, it is enough to know that most of us are using only the left side of our brain right now. We are trained to use this side of the brain almost exclusively and this area deals with reason, logic, analysis and judgement. The left side of our brain deals with objects and differences, comparisons and functions to help us move around in the world.

What most of us don't know is that the left side of the brain can contain some limited ways of thinking that do not allow us to access forgiving thoughts. When we use this side of the brain we will find it hard to forgive others and we may even find it difficult to want to forgive. This part of our brain is interested in our survival and security and as such can see traits like kindness and forgiveness as weak or even pointless.

We will look at what the right side of the brain does and how to access it in the next lesson.

Reason 4 — We feel we should want to forgive for selfless reasons.

In spiritual groups or circles, forgiveness has been thought of as a selfless thing to do; we might feel we are supposed to want to forgive someone because it is the "right thing to do". We may also feel pressure to forgive someone to make the other person feel better; which only makes us feel worse when we cannot do it.

There is a useful fact that helps to open the door to forgiveness and making it available to everyone no matter where they are starting from right now:

Most people begin to forgive for totally selfish reasons and that is ok! It is completely acceptable and common practice to forgive someone just because you are so tired of feeling hate, anger or judging them. Holding onto these feelings has been described as being like holding onto a hot coal and wondering why you get burnt. At some point we want to drop this heavy burden. It can also cause us to feel burnt out, exhausted, to lose sleep and feel stressed among many more issues.

We are human beings and we are naturally wired to want to feel better. If that is what brings you to look at forgiveness then this is just as valid a reason to start forgiving as any other. I am giving you permission to be totally selfish. In fact the other person who wronged you may never know that you forgave them and you may never see them again. The benefit of forgiving may only be felt in yourself and you deserve to feel better.

Exercises for Lesson One

1 — Make a list of the following areas of your life (and add any that you feel are important):

- Health
- Childhood/growing up
- Finances
- Career
- Spiritual pathway
- Relationship/romance
- Friendships
- Hobbies

For each one write down any "should" and "shouldn't" thoughts you regularly have such as "I should have settled down by now and got married", "I shouldn't have eaten that extra slice of pizza".

Spend some time looking at where you are holding judgements of yourself and unrealistic expectations. Simply acknowledging these will begin to make you feel more accepting. Remember it is not what you want or don't want but where you are "should-ing" and "shouldn't-ing" yourself out of peace.

It is ok to have the occasional thought like "I should have turned right at that junction rather than left" but most of us habitually punish ourselves with these thoughts over and over.

2 — Look at this list for each area and see which ones are unrealistic. If you slow down the time frame for each one, you will come to see you did the best you could and are always doing so. Even if you are somehow unconsciously

sabotaging your chances of promotion at work or a happy marriage; nobody would do this intentionally, so give yourself a break!

If you look honestly and deeply at this list you will find that 90% or more of these are really unfair self-judgements or even impossible asks of yourself. Remember nobody will see this list except you, so spend some time with it and maybe revisit it throughout the course.

CHAPTER 4

The Forgiveness Course Lesson Two
The Science of Forgiving

Introduction

In lesson one we took a brief look at our expectations of ourselves and I asked you to consider them again honestly. Most of us would have to admit at least some of them are unreasonable and that we are expecting too much from ourselves with our "should" and "shouldn't" thoughts. It's easy to say "I shouldn't let the kids get me angry and shout at them" but in the heat of the moment, our biology can take over and our best intentions cannot always help us then.

Often we try to address this by trying harder to control ourselves or to be more forgiving. However until we know how to access our right brain thinking, we may simply keep repeating the same behaviour patterns and end up feeling guilty and powerless to change. Once we know how the two sides of the brain work differently, we can begin to understand ourselves more and why we do the things we do.

We can also begin to forgive others too with this knowledge and so it serves us to spend some time looking at this.

The left side of the brain

The left side of the brain is based on the old animal brain and used by most people almost exclusively. It's developed from the old brain and has the function of assessing differences and qualities of things, making distinctions and value judgements, offering quick and simple guidance (such as run or stay) and more. It analyses the complex amount of sensory data that comes in each moment and uses a set of previously determined beliefs and parameters to decide if something is a threat or not.

This side of our brain has very simple decision making processes. It is capable of making a split second decision about something by weighing the sensory input and measuring it up against what we believe to be true, valuable and valid. It is concerned with survival and seeks to protect our physical body and our mental self-image of who we think we are. The left side of the brain is capable of ignoring any sensory input that contradicts what it knows to be true and it runs on assumptions. For example, we may have had a bad experience with a dog as a child so it will assume for the rest of our life that dogs are dangerous and we will respond with a fear response. We may also not notice or disregard any evidence that comes to us that dogs are friendly and fun. This is an automatic process that occurs in a fraction of a second and usually we don't even have time to think about it consciously.

This side of the brain runs on unconscious decisions and assumptions that have been tried and tested in the world and our experience of life and we must exert effort to overturn or replace one of these assumptions. Note how much willpower it takes to overcome a bad habit; how we tend to view all homeless people the same way for example and how our views of politics, religion and much more seem to be very general and unchanging. People can often get very defensive when their views on things are challenged by others and even some people are willing to die for these beliefs.

The vicious circle of assumption action and belief

The left side of the brain works on logic, reason and rational thinking; however, this rational thinking is often based on unconscious irrational beliefs we are unaware of. For example, we can be trying to lose weight so we choose healthy foods, but we succumb to a takeaway that is full of fat because deep down we believe "no matter what I do, I cannot lose weight." We have the good intention but we see our actions are controlled by deeply rooted beliefs and then our brain gets to see "evidence" that this belief is true. This then serves to reinforce this vicious circle of an assumption about ourselves, others or life in general as we believe, see the evidence of the belief in action and then the mind feels justified in holding this belief.

Every single person at this level is being held hostage by these deeply-rooted beliefs and their actions, words and behaviour comes directly from them; rather than from our logical reasonable thoughts as we would like to believe. Add to this the fact that quite often our emotions overtake us and overrule our rational thinking in times of being tested. Our left brain logical thinking can be short-circuited by strong emotion and we all know that "heat of the moment" feeling.

Forgiveness begins to become possible of ourselves and others when we see that we are often stuck in this cycle of believing something to be true that we do not even know we believe. We then have no choice but to act this belief out and experience the results of it. This produces strong thoughts and emotions and perpetuates the whole cycle.

There are two myths that float around in our consciousness and stop us from being able to forgive. We will expose these now:

- Myth 1 — "Everyone should be able to act, think, understand and speak at the same level I do."

We all deep down feel that our opinions are more valid than the next person's and that our way of doing things is the best way. We believe that just because we are able to see both sides of an argument, for example, both parties involved in the argument should be able to also. Yet both parties firmly believe they are right and cannot consider the other's point of view.

- Myth 2 — "I/they should have done better. I/they shouldn't have said what I/they did."

Our left sided brain really believes in the "should" and "shouldn't" and yet these are simply hypothetical beliefs with no basis in fact.

Explanation

Each person's level of consciousness is vibrating at a certain level and this allows them to think thoughts that vibrate at a level similar to their vibration. Thoughts vibrate at a certain level and in turn attract more thoughts. Our words are simply verbalised thoughts and our actions are extensions of our thoughts and level of consciousness. We may feel as though we are choosing our own actions and thoughts; yet in reality we only have access to thoughts in our own range.

We can see that if we are an angry person, for example, we most likely will find someone that talks about forgiveness and compassion to be strange, misguided and out of touch with "how things really are in the world".

Another example we can see is that some people obviously feel it is ok to kill other people for fun or just to "see what it feels like", such as a serial killer. Yet most of us would never be in the range vibrationally of such thoughts. Some of us may feel it is ok to kill if it is for a noble cause, such as military defence, yet others may feel it is never ok to kill for any reason at all. It is likely that people who feel each of these three ways would consider the other two viewpoints abhorrent and unthinkable.

Each time we think a thought of a certain vibrational range, it is easier and easier to choose a similar thought and make a corresponding action. Each time we choose thoughts of the same frequency we reinforce neural pathways in our brain. It takes effort to choose an unfamiliar thought over a familiar one. It is impossible to choose a higher thought if you do not know you have a choice!

If we consistently choose hateful, angry and unloving thoughts, it will get harder and harder to pull ourselves out of a downward spiral and make a different choice. If we consistently choose forgiving, loving thoughts and seek to understand, we will find it harder and harder to pull ourselves out of an upward spiral.

Every person is stuck in their own personal world of projections about themselves, their world and others. When people talk about you, they are really talking about what they think of you. Our world of opinions, "facts" and beliefs is a virtual world that has no basis in reality at all. Consider now the person that wronged you. They did not have a choice but to act the way they did. To say they should have done differently is a denial of reality. Only once that person knows what you know now and sees they have a choice, will they actually be able to choose differently.

Right side of the brain

The right side of our brain seeks to understand rather than to analyse. It wants to know about how things actually are and not how we think they are (quite often these are completely opposite). This side of the brain takes in all possibilities rather than fixing on one viewpoint only. It can take in more information and is intuitive rather than logical, it tends to sense rather than analyse. This side of the brain looks for the overall context of a situation rather than isolated facts.

The right side of our brain is slower to respond to a stimulus than the left but is less easily overruled by strong emotions. We may face the same challenging situations but be able to keep our cool in the heat of the moment. Most people are sadly unable to access this part of the brain for very long at all, unless they are artists, musicians or other similar people. Even once we can access this higher thinking for a while, we may feel as though we are slipping back and forth from one way to the other. We might find ourselves saying "he really shouldn't have done that" whilst knowing deep down that he had no choice. At a certain level of consciousness, the right brain will always overrule the left brain but for most of humanity, it is the other way around! They have no choice!

We are always operating at whatever level of consciousness we are at. We can only move to a higher one by choice, knowing it is possible to do so, with the right information and help and by effort to establish a new set of beliefs. Once we see this, we will come to know that everyone is always making their highest choice, they are always acting out the highest level of consciousness they have available to them at that moment. Then our "should" and "shouldn't" moments disappear.

It is not that people won't change. It is that they can't!

Doing this course is a right-brained activity as it is encouraging you to understand and know more. Therefore, forgiveness of yourself and others is happening as a by-product of learning this information.

Willingness is the key

You do not actually have to forgive anyone or yourself, you only have to be willing to forgive. When we are willing to forgive, we automatically move to a higher level of consciousness and from this level we can forgive what we could not before.

You are only responsible for achieving a willingness to forgive because the moment you are willing, you are vibrationally saying "I am willing to let go of these particular thoughts and achieve a higher level". Even to say (and mean) "I can't forgive them right now and I don't want to at the moment" is a step towards willingness. The next step is also easy if we can come to say "I would like to be able to forgive them at some point".

Willingness is easy once you see that you must already want to forgive or else you would not be participating in a course like this. Are you willing to forgive right now? If not now, could you be in the future? If yes then your "work" is done. Unwillingness to forgive comes from thinking and believing that people should be able to do better and they cannot. It is not that they won't do better, they can't. Witness your own behaviour when you say something out of anger you immediately regret but cannot take back.

You do not actually need to know how to forgive, it will happen for you as you move to a new level of consciousness. You must only develop the willingness to forgive. You must want to want to forgive.

Even if right now you don't feel willing, to admit that you would like to in the future is the key. That is all you need to be able to do. To develop willingness, you must only come to see that everyone is doing exactly what they are capable of only. They are already living in and acting out their highest level of consciousness. As you are too.

Exercise for Lesson Two

• Make a list of the major "should" and "shouldn't" thoughts you have about other people that may have wronged you recently or anytime in your history. This list can also include anything you have a sense of injustice, bitterness or a strong opinion about how things should be.

Take a moment to review each area of your life as before and see if there are any people you are holding responsible for

29

things that happened to you, are holding a grudge against or feel angry, bitter or hurt by. You can also include anyone that has hurt someone you love.

This can be an emotional process and you can take your time doing this.

• Now divide your list into two sections labelled "A — Willing to forgive right now" and "B — Unwilling to forgive right now".

• For A, spend a moment mentally releasing any thoughts or feelings about each one and choose privately to access higher thoughts and feelings about each one. (This will be done for you but you must give permission).

• For B, consider why you are unwilling to forgive right now. If you are able to be honest when you look, you will most likely find that some "should" or "shouldn't" thoughts are still being believed. If you can let go of them, do it and choose to be free of the pain of thinking those thoughts. If you cannot let go of them put a star next to any that you want to be able to forgive.

• Recognise your intention and willingness to forgive soon is the highest choice you could have made in this moment and you have done all that you need to.

Note — for items on list B, it is a good idea to revisit them after a few days and re-examine any "should" and "shouldn't" thoughts and recheck your willingness to forgive now. You may be surprised!

30

Sometimes simply knowing you don't have to forgive at all right now softens the resistance to doing it anyway. It is your choice to hold onto the hot coal for the rest of your life and maybe get burnt. It's certainly not true that you "should" have forgiven by now.

If you could forgive, you would have and the moment you can, you will do.

CHAPTER 5

The Forgiveness Course Lesson Three

Immunising Yourself Against Further Hurt

Introduction

In this lesson, we are going to take a look at why someone's actions, words or ideas about us can seem to hurt us. We will analyse this process of what actually happens and in doing so enable ourselves to come to a realisation that will stop any further hurt from occurring. This process will involve us moving to a higher level of consciousness and is simple to understand once you have the correct information. As always in this course, we are going to learn the correct information and allow that to facilitate a shift to a higher level of consciousness.

There is a level of consciousness in which some people live every day that cannot be hurt or wronged by anyone else. This may sound incredible and impossible but I would ask you to keep an open mind as you read through this lesson and come to see for yourself. Imagine if you can, what it would be like to move through the world knowing that nothing anyone can do to you or say about you could hurt you. Wouldn't you automatically be more at peace and happier if this was how you were living?

This understanding will also allow you to have more time, energy and patience for other people too. There is no need to worry that if you are beyond being able to be hurt by others that you will seem cold, uncaring or selfish; in fact you may find yourself more popular than ever.

Understanding why we feel hurt when someone wrongs us

This might seem like the most obvious and pointless thing to explore because we have been raised to believe that the actions, words and behaviour of others can have an impact on us. This is simply not true and let's now expose another myth that we have come to believe very deeply and without question:

• Myth — "Other people can do and say things that can harm or cause injury to me; either my physical body or my sense of self"

To understand why this is not true we need to explore what we actually think of as ourselves. Most people feel that they are:

1. Their physical body
2. Their emotions
3. Their thoughts/ideas about themselves, others and the world in general.

All of this together is what most of us assume is "me" and it's never questioned. We also believe that this is all that we are — that we are a body and mind and that there is nothing else to us that is more permanent. We will look at what we really are in lesson four but for now we can focus on the aspects of ourselves listed above.

If we really look at number 3 on that list, it is really a collection of thoughts only. It is a set of ideas of what we think is true about ourselves. These thoughts are so deeply believed by ourselves that we no longer question them for the most part. These thoughts range from thoughts about our physical body, to thoughts about our psychological self and have often been called "projections".

An example of such a projection is "I am a woman and I am 32 years old". This is really a statement about your body and not about you!

Another example of a projection is "I am a good person, I try my hardest to be kind to other people". This is really a statement about what you believe about your psychological self or your mind. It is really describing what thoughts you often have about yourself rather than your actual self.

35

Our projections about ourselves are who we think we are.

We are so identified with these projections about ourselves, that if I stopped ten people on the street and ask them to describe themselves they would probably describe what their physical body is like, but they would say "I am male/female". If pressed for more detail, eventually they would begin to describe their minds and not themselves, but again they would say "I like learning French and I love Chinese food".

Caught up in these projections are what we want for ourselves and how we would like our life to unfold so that we feel happy.

Not only do we have projections about ourselves, but we also have them about other people, events, the world in general and more.

We may have a mental picture of what we think someone is like and we are convinced that it is true. One neighbour might try to take your parking space so you built an image of them in your mind that they are mean and rude. Yet another neighbour may invite that same person round to their house and be very good friends with them and have a mental image that they are a very kind person and a good friend.

We must come to see that our projections about others and ourselves are in no way true. They are subjective and often differ based on what we experience in the moment. We would all like to think that our ideas are the truth, but they are a virtual world that exists only inside our head. Sometimes, in the case of social causes, religion, media, politics and others, we can have thousands of people agreeing with our projections and we feel even more justified in having them.

The key to forgiveness

A major key to being able to forgive anyone of anything is to see that people cannot actually hurt us; they can only hurt our projections about ourselves or others. Everyone is stuck in their own projections, believing them to be reality and believing that everyone else has the same projections. If we believe that we are our projections, then we will feel injured by anything that threatens our projections.

We will look at some examples to illustrate this point:

Example 1 — You are happily engaged to be married to someone you love very much and you find out your best friend has been seeing your fiancé without your knowledge. You feel furious, hurt, betrayed and unable to forgive your friend and your fiancé.

Most people would believe here that the fiancé and this friend have done something that has hurt them completely. But if we really slow down and take a look at what is happening here we will see that the actions of the fiancé and friend have destroyed the projection that "I am going to be married to this person and we will live a long and happy life together."

It has also destroyed the idea that you and this best friend will stay friends forever.

Example 2 — You lent your friend some money to help when they lost their job and couldn't pay their bills. You told your friend that you needed the money back by a certain date and now that date has elapsed and they have not paid you back. You needed that money to pay a bill of your own and so you go to see the friend and tell them you need your money back today. When you get to your friend's house, you see that they have used the money for other things in the house and they do not seem to be as needy as they have implied.

In a flash, you see that they have lied to you about why they needed the money and perhaps knew a while ago that they could not pay it back, or worse that they had no intention of giving it back. Now you are in trouble because you need that money to pay your bills this month and there is nothing you can do to get it back.

Now you may feel that they have hurt you by not telling you the truth sooner, or even perhaps deliberately misleading you to get money from you and you cannot forgive them for that. We can look more closely to see that there was a projection about that particular friend that they were trustworthy, honest and fair and this has been destroyed by their actions. You may also have had a projection about yourself that you are always a good judge of character and knew that lending the money was the right thing to do. There could also be a projection too that you are a good person and that if you help others, they will help you.

Again, all these projections are crushed by these actions.

Even if a person does something to hurt your physical body, they really cannot hurt you. They are hurting your projections that you will live a long and healthy life, or that the person that injured you is nice, kind and would never do anything to hurt you. This may seem hard to understand at first but if we look at why we look after our physical body we will see that if it is in good health we have projections that we will live longer, feel better and experience more. Anything that damages our body will feel bad because it has damaged our projection about our longevity and health.

You are not your body or your mind; you are the Witness of both of these. Nothing can hurt you unless you choose to believe that you are your mind and its projections. Even then it will only seem to hurt you.

Now that you know this you have a choice. You need never be hurt by the actions or words of others or yourself. It becomes your choice whether to believe you are being hurt, or to know your ideas and expectations about others are being hurt.

Expectations, projections or ideas are just thoughts and thoughts cannot really be hurt. Through the actions of others we can come to see that our thoughts about our world, ourselves and others are not as true as we would like to have believed. We may even be forced to admit they are not true at all. Once this realisation really deepens in your consciousness, you will come to see that you can live from this place where you never get hurt again by anything that life can throw at you. Even if someone deliberately set out to cause you emotional pain you can now see that it is not possible.

Only we can cause ourselves to suffer if we insist on believing that we are our thoughts. We have a mind but we are not that mind; it works for us as a functionality but it can only think about things. Our mind's thoughts about reality are not the same as the actual reality.

Exercises for Lesson Three

Take a look back at lists "A" and "B" you made in lesson two. For each one, see if you can identify what projection you had at the time that was hurt by the actions of the people involved.

If you find this difficult to do for some of them that is ok and this does not have to be done all at once. Seeing our projections can be a strange experience and liberating and shocking at the same time. It is enough for now that you are coming to see that the reason the things on your lists hurt is because it threatens the mental image you have or had about yourself and the world.

As we said in lesson two, our left brain works on assumptions and beliefs about ourselves and our environment. It makes decisions based on these assumptions and when they are threatened it can feel as though our centre of focus or our compass has been lost. We have all felt that feeling in the pit of our stomach when something happens that absolutely crushes our assumptions about life.

This lesson has been successful if it has brought you to see that you have assumptions and projections that you believed were you and that only those can be damaged. You cannot be damaged ever.

With reflection on the information in this lesson, you will come to see that nothing can hurt you at all. No person, situation or authority can hurt you and they never have been able to. For the rest of your life you will never be hurt again nor can you hurt others accidentally or by deliberate effort.

One who sees he is not his projections is free from pain and suffering forever.

CHAPTER 6

The Forgiveness Course Lesson Four
The Real Cause of Unforgiveness

Introduction

In this fourth and final lesson of the course, we will look at how we complete this process of forgiveness. We have made amazing strides so far in our journey to forgiving and by now you should be seeing and feeling the benefits of moving beyond what has held you back. There is a final stage to the forgiveness process to complete your understanding of yourself, others, and why humans often behave in ways which can leave us feeling vulnerable and hurt. As always throughout this course, we will learn some new information and begin to use it to rise to a new level of consciousness where we will be able to forgive effortlessly.

The "original sin" and the "fall from grace"

We may have all heard of the "original sin" or the "fall from grace" that has been given a negative meaning by some cultures and religious authorities. There is an idea that there is something inherently wrong in the human psyche that has caused us to be wrong somehow. This idea is so deeply rooted in our culture, that most of us grow up with some amount of self-esteem issues and feel guilty deep down for something that we don't even understand or remember.

If we look at the original meaning of the word "sin" we can see it is derived from Latin and Hebrew words that mean "to miss the mark" or "to be ignorant". It can also have a meaning that something was done unintentionally. We can learn from this that any flaws that humans may have are species-wide and nobody is exempt from this. We must begin to look at how we feel about ourselves with greater clarity. We must stop believing that we fell out of heaven someone not quite up to the standard. We can come to see we do not need to earn a place in heaven, nirvana or whatever your particular beliefs are. We are perfect as we are; our flaws are inherent in the way we are designed and they have to be so.

We didn't fall from grace; we emerged out of love. All is as it should be.

Human potential

Human beings are unique in the world because we have the ability to think and have complex thoughts about ourselves and others. Our brains are much more evolved than most other species and as such, we have the ability to choose our behaviour, words and actions based upon our level of consciousness. We are also the only species that has the ability to question what we are, why we exist, where we came from and other spiritual and important questions.

With the possibility for these evolved thoughts also came the opposite; the highest and lowest behaviours of all human beings can be seen on planet Earth. Most of the lowest behaviours make the daily news headlines. To understand why human beings behave in ways that animals would not, helps us to begin to forgive in an even deeper way.

Left brain function leads to separation thinking

We have learnt before that most human beings can only access the left side of their brain on a regular basis and that this side is responsible for keeping us safe by measuring differences, analysing information quickly, making value judgements and assigning meaning to an experience or person. It is derived from the old animal primitive brain which is instinctive and works on the "fight-or-flight" mechanism to decide if something is a threat, something to be pursued and eaten or a potential mate.

In order for the left brain to function correctly and to make a quick decision, it must be able to instantly judge the difference between itself and the thing it is perceiving. As animals evolved from simple organisms to more complex animals, this left brain function became more evolved also and at its peak has evolved into the human brain and all of its ability to function as we know it.

Our left side of the brain will immediately assume the thing it is perceiving is "other" than itself. We have all become used to the idea that we are separate human beings, that we are this body that we live in and we are alone, walking around in a world that contains other people, animals, plants and inanimate objects. Our view of life is so familiar to us that we may never even question if it is still valid. Of course, we all take for granted the idea that "I am me, this person" so much, that we also assume everyone else is their own person too. We may even have many projections about the other people in our lives too.

We are not actually separate from anything or anyone.

This may seem to be an incredible claim but we can prove it right now. If we look for ourselves we will not find anything that we can call "me". Have a look right now and see if you can find yourself; a well-defined entity called "me" that has a shape and solidity. You will not find anything!

What we are is not a thing at all, we are not separate people; we are the One Being that is expressing itself as all of us in unique but not separate ways. Only our bodies are separate. Separation was never true — it only seemed to be so because we think from our left brains.

If we are willing to look and absorb the truth, we will consistently find that we are not what we thought we are. We will find a kind of space-like feeling, an emptiness or nothingness. This can be scary at first when you first notice it but I urge you to be brave and keep looking. You have always been this formless "no-thing". You do not have a shape or definable qualities like your body. You do not age or die, you were never born.

What you really are is infinite, formless awareness. You are the intelligent principle that animates the body, you are the source of the life-force energy. This formless awareness cannot be separate, it cannot be sliced into "many" beings. There can only be many human bodies but only one Being.

How does this knowledge help us forgive?

When we begin to see that there is nobody else than us, it can begin to end all fear. As humans all of our actions are guided by this root fear that we are isolated and alone and there are many others that could hurt us. All of our beliefs, actions and words come from this deep down sense that we need to protect ourselves from dangers that exist "out there". Our animal brain tends to analyse anything that seems to be "other than me", in case it is something dangerous and is always on some level of alert. Consider the simple way we startle when someone steps up behind us and we were unaware of their presence.

We can begin to see that the actions of every human being are by nature self-serving and narcissistic. That does not make them wrong! It's natural that every person would want to do whatever it takes to survive and that is also true for every animal and plant we see. As human beings, our mind, beliefs and collection of projections about ourselves and others are also classed as "things that I need to protect" by the left brain. They are included in our sense of self; what we think we are. We would not have survived to evolve into the Homo sapiens that we are today, if we had not protected ourselves. That instinctive survival trait is inbuilt in everything we do as a human being and we are usually incapable of doing anything else.

As humans our sense of self includes all that we think about ourselves, others and our world. If we perceive that those thoughts and beliefs are being attacked or threatened, we move to defend them just as we would an attack on our body. We treat an attack upon our projections as just as serious as an attack on our body. This may seem incredible but if you look at the start of every war you will find that someone's projections were threatened. Only later were our actual bodies threatened or harmed. Our projections are so highly-valued and prized that we would risk our bodies to defend them. Until we reach a certain level of consciousness we are incapable of distinguishing between our body and our projections.

Most human beings believe that they are their thoughts and without them they will die. As incredible as this may sound, it is true.

When love begins to prevail

When we begin to access right brain thinking we are capable of actions, thoughts and speech that we were not before. We are able to try to understand, to put things into context and make a decision from a more informed place, rather than a quick analysis and decision based on how it appears things are. The urge to understand is really the emergence of love and this is a consequence of using this side of our brain more.

Only once we have been able to access this side of the brain can we begin to see that actions taken to defend our projections will probably have a negative impact on others. We are finally able to consider the needs of others above ourselves. This is a skill that a large percentage of the human population does not yet have. It begins to emerge with parenthood and we can see how a mother or father will sacrifice themselves for their child without a thought. This is the first time we see such behaviour in the animal and human kingdom.

Moving on from always thinking of our needs and wants, we can begin to consider others also in our plans and desires. The final evolution of humanity, however, is to realise there are no others at all. That was simply an illusion caused by perceiving life through the left side of the brain and living in a world of "me and everyone else".

When we live from a level of consciousness where we know deeply that all we see and perceive is us, our actions begin to change; our words and deeds begin to be loving and wise. We would of course still take action to stop someone from hurting us or someone we love but we would do it only when necessary. At this level humans are capable of love, compassion, charity and selfless service to other human beings. Innate in the awareness that "All is us" is the idea that everyone is equal and yet unique. Everyone is deserving of our love and that their actions may come from a limited place at the moment but they have no other choice.

Everyone is acting out of a very real seeming fear and they cannot help it. We must come to see that as humans evolve and the idea that they are separate loses its power, then our actions as a race will change too. Until then we can begin to have compassion for those stuck at lower levels of consciousness because they have no choice but to keep making the same errors of judgement based upon the faulty premise that "I am this body and when it dies so do I".

Conclusion

What you have learnt in this course will give you a solid foundation to begin to forgive deeply. To forgive yourself and others is really to forgive humanity for being limited in some ways. Limited but not wrong.

Unconditional love will begin to emerge naturally from digesting what you have absorbed and applied. Unconditional love does not mean that you blindly accept the actions of others; but rather that you love a person for what they really are, a human being limited by brain function, fear and a self-protective urge. Being human affords us the highest and lowest of choices each and every moment. What we choose to do and say is limited by our previous choices and it often takes someone with a higher level of consciousness to facilitate new choices. We can all be that guiding light for each other. When we do, we will move from unconditional love to Oneness which is the highest form of love there is. Oneness does not see any separation at all and sees only ourselves wherever we look. We all inherently love ourselves and want to survive and we will encourage all of humanity to do this as we evolve.

Eventually our sense of self will encompass the whole universe if allowed to and life really can be quite magical from there. Just as we have needed to make all of our previous errors in judgement in order to evolve to where we are now; so too we would not begrudge any other being from having the same learning experiences.

It is only by making mistakes that we can choose a higher choice next time.

Exercises for Lesson Four

1. See if you can indeed find yourself when you look. You will find your body, mind and emotions but where are you?
2. See if you can describe yourself as this formless awareness. Find out if you have an edge or boundary.

3. Contemplate that if you cannot find an end to the formless you then you must be everywhere and everything.

4. Re-read through all the previous exercises and make a note of any areas you still cannot forgive. Note that there is no other person to forgive. Ask for help if you need it from any Divine source or from myself or others in the course. An unwillingness to forgive is really an unwillingness to evolve and flourish into your highest possible expression you are capable of right now. It is a desire to hold onto a belief in "me and others". Is it worth losing the peace, love and joy that naturally emerge from living as the One Being?

Thank you for loving yourself enough to participate in this course. This is not the end but a beginning of possibility for you!

SECTION TWO

CHAPTER 7

Transcending the Vasanas Course

Introduction

Transcending the vasanas has been viewed by some spiritual cultures as taking many lifetimes and being very difficult to do; this may have been the case in the past but not anymore. This course will help you do it much easier and faster and you will begin to see more peace, joy and a growing sense of freedom each week you participate. We will use a combination of the correct information, a deeper insight into how our mind works and simple exercises to begin to undo these patterns that disturb our peace.

We will follow a step-by-step process and break down the vasanas into 6 easy to understand stages. In each lesson we will look at two stages of the process. The exercises are designed to help begin the transcendence process and allow you to fully utilise the information you are given in each lesson. I would urge you to complete these exercises as fully as you can.

You can participate in this course no matter where you are in your spiritual journey. You do not need to have knowledge of any particular spiritual pathway or practice and you do not need to be an expert meditator. All you need is some time each week, a pen and paper and a commitment to completing this course.

CHAPTER 8

Transcending the Vasanas Course Lesson One
Stage One and Two

Introduction

In this course we are going to be identifying which vasanas are operating in our lives and then begin to disassemble them stage by stage. These vasanas are simply where our mind has become confused by a false idea and is unable to recognise that it is not true. It is as if you were trying to get somewhere with a faulty GPS system, although you did not know it was not working properly.

In each stage we will highlight how the vasana will be presenting itself to you so that you can recognise it. Then we will look at the false idea for each stage so that we can begin to undo it. Once you see that an idea is not true it automatically begins to stop the idea being believed and begins to loosen the hold of the vasana.

Each time we dissolve a vasana you will notice more clarity, more energy and peace in your life.

There are a few important points to note before we begin:

1. Each vasana will need to be looked at from the stage it is at and worked backwards, until it dissolves into nothingness (don't worry, I will show you how to do that).

2. Each time a vasana is ready to be transcended at the next level, it will appear back in your life again and it will present itself exactly the same way. If you do not know this, you may feel that you have not been successful in transcending the previous stage. (This will become clearer as we go through each lesson)

3. When you work on any vasana or mind pattern that you have, you are simultaneously working on them all. So the more you do the easier it gets. At some point the noisy mind will unravel itself and there will be peace. Just like with an old worn out garment, if you know which loose thread to pull, you can unravel the whole garment at once.

4. Each vasana you have will be showing itself to you either physically (as a situation that keeps on manifesting in your world), emotionally (as a strong emotional response that can often feel a disproportionately large response to the situation that triggered it), mentally (as a barrage of repetitive thoughts that come after a trigger) or spiritually (as

a deeply-rooted subconscious belief). With the help of this course you can recognise them and begin to dissolve them.

5. Vasanas are dissolved or transcended by contemplating the false idea in each stage and finding out if it is actually true. Our noisy mind is held together by assumptions only. Once we begin to question these we will find they dissolve quickly.

Let's begin!

Stage One — The trigger event in the world.

Some of our vasanas will be presenting themselves in our outer world, manifesting themselves as a certain person, situation or event that seems to cause us to feel a great amount of negative emotion on a regular basis. We may experience the same trigger many times and feel a lot of emotion such as anger, fear, irritation etc. There may also be many repetitive thoughts.

We may feel that the event, situation or person is the cause of our discomfort and have spent a great deal of time and energy trying to change things in our outside world to feel better.

This stage is easy to recognise because it is usually characterised by something we want, need or don't want anymore. We may have something happen which causes a lack of money, time, respect, love or other things.

Examples of physically manifesting vasanas

1. A family member you know well keeps upsetting you by saying things about you that are not true. You feel stuck because it just seems like a joke to them but they do not realise you are getting angry and upset each time. You have tried to stop this by talking to them and asking them to stop but to no effect, you even felt worse after talking it through as they could not understand why you were hurting.

2. You go to the ATM and find there is not enough money in the account as you thought there should be. When you check you realise you have overspent and you have a sudden feeling of panic and worry about how you will survive the rest of the month financially. You see a pattern where you keep doing this but you cannot seem to make it stop.

The vasana is being sustained at this stage by false idea 1:

False idea 1 — I can change the outside world to get what I want and to make me feel better.

We must begin to see that the cause of our issues and challenges are due to an internal energy field with which we are approaching these issues. We are so powerful that whatever we are believing to be true we will experience; we are the cause of our world but not in a personal sense. When things are not going well it is because we are holding a lower energy field about a situation, person or thing perhaps unconsciously. These energy fields are just frequencies made up of the thoughts and emotions based on the false ideas we are now exposing.

In order to transcend this stage we must come to see that whatever actions we take to try and change the trigger event in the world will be largely ineffective because we have not raised our energy field as yet.

As we begin to understand this we realise we must also take inner action too.

Exercises for Stage One

1. Write down all the situations, events and issues you have in your life that keep repeating over and over. They may repeat once a year or once a month. Be sure to include all the ones you would like to change or stop from happening. These can include things that you feel you are doing wrong or that someone else is doing wrong to you. They can also be situations where you never seem to have enough time, money, patience etc.

2. Next to each one write down all the actions and things you have been doing to try to improve the situation. For example if you keep overspending, as in example 2 above, you might be trying to budget better, keeping better records and trying to earn more money or get a promotion.

3. Recognise that all the actions you are taking internally or externally to help improve the situation are not wrong, they may be entirely appropriate actions for the situation. If you are spending too much, of course you will want to try to spend less. Here we are not saying that we should stop trying to fix the issues in the outer world; rather we are saying we should also add some inner work to it too or else it will not bear fruit.

4. Accept that it is not your fault that you cannot fix these issues from what you have been trying to do. Until you had the information that these issues are showing themselves in the world outside of us but have roots and causes within our being, you could not have fixed them.

Stage Two — The inner response

With a little inner searching we can come to see that the trigger event is not really what is upsetting us; rather it is the inner response of repetitive, nonsense thoughts caused by the trigger that are causing us to suffer and we try to make it stop.

We can know this to be true if we look closer at the trigger events themselves. We may have had similar issues in the past and we were not disturbed by it. We can also see that if the trigger event was the cause of our unease and disturbance, it should affect every human being equally but it does not. Some people can go through similar trigger events and seem completely peaceful and others can feel absolutely distraught at the same occurrence. We can come to see that what upsets us is not the thing itself but how we respond to it.

We can also notice that there are things that used to upset us that no longer do now and so we can conclude that it cannot ever have been the event itself that caused us pain, or else we would have never let anything go.

We can recognise that with each trigger event comes a barrage of thoughts about it that are usually not helpful, repetitive in nature and really just a lot of thoughts about why this should or shouldn't have happened. It is these thoughts that upset us and not the event itself.

The vasana is being held in place by the idea that we can push away these thoughts and that will make them stop.

False idea — I can do something with these thoughts to make them go away. I can reject them or accept them.

We can transcend this stage by seeing the thoughts caused by the trigger are really what is upsetting us. We can also begin to see that along with the thoughts, comes an urge to resist or to accept the thoughts too. This is really just two more thoughts that say "I don't want or like these thoughts" or "I like these thoughts".

There is nothing we can do about the thoughts coming and there is nothing we can about the urge to accept or resist them. We can simply witness the thoughts and urges come and go. When we simply watch the thoughts we allow them to come and go and we are not disturbed.

Here are the examples we looked at earlier showing themselves at this stage.

Examples of mentally manifesting vasanas

Example 1 — You begin to see there have been times that the family member has said things about you that did not bother you at all. Other people can say things that do not hurt you. You begin to realise it is all the thoughts that come that are upsetting you. Thoughts such as "people are going to believe what they are saying" and "It is so unfair what they are saying", or "I hate it when they lie about me" are the cause of your pain.

Example 2 — You go to the ATM again and there is little money left after you have overspent again. Immediately there is a lot of "what am I going to do now?" thoughts and a lot of self-blaming thoughts. After these thoughts come a whole lot of thoughts about not being good enough and you end up feeling very angry at yourself. You can begin to see that it is not the lack of money that is upsetting you because you have been in worse situations before and survived. It is the attacking thoughts that have come and keep coming that you are hurt by and are trying to push away.

Exercises for Stage Two

1. For each of the vasanas you wrote down in stage one exercises, make a list of the type of thoughts that come after the trigger event happens. They can be thoughts you want to have and like and thoughts you try to push away. In example 2 above, you may have thoughts such as "why have I done this yet again?" that make you feel bad and you push them away. You may also have empowering thoughts that you want to keep like "next time I won't let this happen again".

2. Note down whether these are thoughts you either try to push away or hold onto.

3. Accept that you are able to make a third choice which is simply to watch the thoughts come and go. You do not have to engage any urge to do anything with the thoughts.

4. Make a commitment that when the trigger event next happens, you will remain in a neutral stance mentally and simply observe the thoughts and urges. Of course you can still go about your life; it is a good idea to practice witnessing thoughts as you go about your day.

CHAPTER 9

Transcending the Vasanas Course Lesson Two
Stage Three and Four

Introduction

In lesson one we have highlighted and begun to work on
the vasanas we can see in our lives that are manifesting
either:

1. In our outer world as a situation, event or person that
    keeps troubling us or
2. In our mind as repetitive thoughts about a situation
    that come again and again.

We also began to work on these vasanas to bring them
back to their more subtle forms. Each time we work on a
vasana, we will see it become clearer and easier to identify
as it begins to heal from our outer world and mind and
moves inwards. At each stage we will be able to work on the
vasanas faster and in a much easier way.

Stage Three — The emotional response

We are now going to identify the deeper root of the issues we highlighted in lesson one. The outer trigger event and the inner response of noisy thoughts are really being caused by a build-up of repressed emotional charge within our being. As human beings nobody has told us how to actually feel our emotions. This may seem like a strange idea but we have little to no education in this subject. We all grow up and learn to handle emotions by either suppressing them deep down inside us, projecting them "out there" into our outer world and blaming others for how we feel, or expressing them in an extreme way (such as road rage).

We are taught to believe that our emotions are caused by events that happen in our lives, when in reality it is the other way around.

The trigger event and the repetitive thoughts are being caused and attracted by the emotions we haven't been able to feel as yet. They are a symptom of the emotional charge that has not been dissipated.

We must identify which emotions we feel on a regular basis and allow ourselves to feel them when they come up. Feeling them is allowing the energy of them to manifest in our body and last as long as it needs to, then to discharge itself.

There are two false ideas at this stage:

1. **If I don't allow myself to feel this emotion, it will go away and I won't have to deal with it.**
2. **Also, if I allow myself to feel this emotion, it will overwhelm me and it will be unpleasant or I will not be able to shut it off again.**

Both of these are ways that we avoid actually feeling the emotion, without realising it.

Exercises for Stage Three

1. For each of the physically manifesting vasanas you wrote down for stage one write a list of the emotions that you feel regularly when the trigger event happens. Be sure to include any emotions that come each time. It can be sadness, fear, irritation, anger or anything at all. It might actually only feel like a sense of overwhelm rather than any particular emotions you can identify.
2. Referring to the list you wrote for stage two of thoughts that come again and again; write a list of emotions that you feel when these thoughts come. You only need to write down any emotions that you feel that you have not already highlighted in exercise 1 above.
3. Recognise that you have not fully allowed yourself to feel each emotion on the two lists above. If you had done, they would not come back each time a trigger

happens, or thoughts come. They are coming asking for you to feel them. Remember it is safe to feel how you feel. If you are willing to feel the emotion fully, even for a few minutes, you are allowing some of the excess charge to dissipate and you will begin to feel lighter and happier. Nothing bad will happen to you if you feel a strong negative emotion; you may notice an increasing sense of self-confidence and self-esteem when you begin to feel these emotions and allow them.

4. Each time these emotions come, you must allow them to come and be felt until the excess of emotional energy has been allowed to leave. This may go on for a few weeks or months, where the emotion periodically comes back for apparently no reason.

Stage Four — The assumptions of mind

In this stage, we will begin to look at the hidden beliefs that are causing the previous stage of vasanas. The emotions we are feeling are caused by a belief that we have not investigated as yet. These beliefs are not true and cause us to suffer but we have believed them for so long, we are not conscious that they are still operating within us.

When we believe a thought, we will have a large and well-established neuro pathway for it in our brain. When that thought runs through our brain it produces a large neurochemical response. This neurochemical then in turn floods our system and causes an emotional reaction in the body.

In this stage, we will use the emotions we feel to reveal what hidden belief we are still assuming to be true. We can simply ask each emotion what it is trying to tell us. Each emotion vibrates on a certain frequency and is trying to tell us that we are believing something that is not true (if it is a negative emotion).

Here are the false ideas that hold us back in this stage:

1 — These beliefs I have are true and there is nothing I can do about them.

2 — I have had these beliefs so long that it will be too painful to look at them.

3 — Suppressing or projecting these beliefs makes them go away and I am unaffected by them.

The only way for us to release these beliefs once and for all is to contemplate the truth of them. We must first accept that some part of us is still believing them or else we would not be feeling the emotion. Then we can reveal the belief and question if it is true.

These beliefs are held in place when we assume the belief is true. When we question whether it is actually true, we can come to sense an opening or a shift in our consciousness as we realise they have never been true.

You may notice that it is hard to remember to question the beliefs and most times you have believed the thought before you even realise what has happened. Don't worry, this is normal and it is important to note that your intention to question them is key and it will remind you more and more to question them in the moment. Intention is very important and all powerful in this spiritual journey.

Exercises for Stage Four

1. For each of the emotions you listed in the previous stage make a heading on a sheet of paper, such as "Guilt" and "Fear" and leave some room. Ask the emotion what it is trying to tell you, what story it is holding onto and feel within yourself as you ask. When you have hit upon the right belief you will know, it will have some subtle feeling along with it. You may feel angst or tension as you consider this belief. If you are not sure if you have hit the right belief, ask me for help.

2. Double check each emotion, as it may have two or three hidden beliefs underneath.

3. Also ask for a hidden belief behind any feelings of overwhelm again.

4. For each belief ask yourself if it is really true. This is important. Ask in an open and curious way. All of us have simply assumed it is true. We may have statements written down that have plagued our life and been our inner tormentor, such as "I am not good

enough" or "I am not safe" or "I am never going to be good enough". Most people have a deep sense of unworthiness and feel unsafe at the core of their being. This can be shocking at first but it is safe to see it now because you have the tools to undo it. You have always been good enough, safe and loved and now you can stop manifesting situations through these vasanas that agree with the beliefs. Instead you will begin to see more and more evidence that you are perfect, whole, safe and loved.

5. Don't stop your contemplative questioning until you feel an experiential shift in your consciousness. Most of us will receive thought answers first when we ask if a belief is true. Then we will receive an emotional answer. Next and most importantly, we will begin to receive an answer that is not in words or a feeling; rather it will be a sense of opening, relief, lightening or release. You will feel as if something heavy has left you and you are clearer than before. There may also be a sense that the belief is so obviously not true; so much so that you cannot understand how you ever thought it was true!

For more information on contemplative techniques please see my book "Transcending the Mind-Some Disassembly Required".

Be sure that you have looked at every belief that you wrote. There may be similar ones that no longer seem relevant after you have looked at a few but check anyway. Your mind is sneaky and it will be looking for a way out of changing right now.

If you are in any doubt if you have the right belief, please ask me. It is vital to get the right ones at this stage if we are to heal the vasanas.

CHAPTER 10

Transcending the Vasanas Course Lesson Three
Stage Five

Introduction

In this lesson we are only going to look at one stage only; stage five is a fundamental stage and as such is worth slowing down and taking more time on it. The false idea in this stage is the underpinning of all the others and as such, is a very direct way to heal and transcend. Because of this we may notice more resistance to this stage inside ourselves.

Stage Five — The belief in separation

In each previous stage of this book we were working on the assumption that you are separate, alone in the universe; that you are this body and it is all that you are. We were coming from the idea that whatever happens to your body is happening to you and that when it dies so will you. Now we will move to a much higher viewpoint and begin to make a huge leap in consciousness.

In this stage we will work on a vital assumption of the mind that is at the core of all our suffering as a human. We all believe deep down that we are separate beings. We believe that we are this body and mind and that is all we are. This belief is so pervasive throughout humans that we never usually stop to question it. If we take a look at how we came to believe this, we can see that it is a normal part of our development. At first, we are the formless awareness and when a body appears in it, then we can naturally become fascinated with it and how it works. We start to entertain thoughts about what we are and what is "mine". We hold onto our body, mind and emotions as "mine" and because of this, we fear the end of our body as being the end of us.

Most of us believe so deeply that we are this body, that we are affected by everything that happens in the body and to it. In this stage we will look at how to see the truth and how to undo this core assumption. Once we can see that our body is a part of us, as is our mind, then we need not fear the death of the body. Once we know that we are here before and beyond the body, then we can live from a higher place of peace and joy.

All of our problems and suffering stem from this belief that we are separate people. We feel so strongly that we are only this body and that we need things from other people to make us happy. The moment we believe we are alone and isolated from others, then we will feel driven to attain whatever we seem to need to feel happy, safe and secure again. The things we need can be tangible things like money, friends, a good job etc or it can be intangible things such as enlightenment, respect, a relationship or more.

All of our interactions with others are affected by what we think we need from them. If we can come to see that we are not separate from others at all and that we are all expressions of the Self, then we will feel complete. We will know that we need nothing to be happy, peaceful and content. No matter what occurs in our lives we will be at peace.

The very moment we start to question our mind's main assumption that we are a person, alone in time and space, travelling through this lifetime and trying to accumulate as much as possible in the time that we have, we will begin to feel better.

The moment we start to transcend this belief we will see all our problems start to disappear. As amazing as it may seem, it is no longer possible to have a problem when you are not a separate being, but are the Wholeness itself.

The vasana is being sustained at this stage by 3 false ideas:

- **I am a separate person; I am me.**
- **I am this mind and body and nothing else.**
- **Everything that happens to the mind and body are happening to me.**

To begin to undo this most basic of assumptions, we must be willing to examine this belief by looking directly at what we are. We can use a guided process of "Self-Inquiry" to look deeper. Each time we assume we are a separate being, we will suffer but each time we actually stop, look and see that we are not separate we will feel better.

Self-Inquiry will actually show us that we are not separate at all; in fact we are not a solid being as we might have thought we were. You may be surprised to find out that you are actually not a thing! You are formless, you have no tangible substance, although your body, thoughts and emotions do. Self-Inquiry is really just the process of looking, trying to find yourself and failing to find a "me" that is here. When we actually stop to look we find a human body, thoughts, emotions and a sense of "me" that is looking; but we will not actually find anything tangible that we can call "me".

At first this discovery can be quite shocking but if you can continue to look you can begin to benefit in a huge way.

What does it mean if you cannot find yourself?

This is such a profoundly different way of viewing yourself to what we are used to that it can take some time to come to terms with and to understand that it is a very good thing.

Let's try to shortcut that process now:

If you cannot find yourself as a tangible thing it means that you must be intangible, formless and yet still just as much present as all the forms in you.

If you are intangible it means:

- You cannot be hurt
- You cannot suffer
- You cannot die because you were never born.
- You do not need anything (your body does of course but not you).
- You can never age or become ill.
- You are already beyond the mind and the vasanas! The vasanas are happening in the manifest reality and world and you are unmanifest in your truest sense of yourself. You are also the manifest too of course.
- You are not separate to anyone else! Nobody else is a tangible someone either.

There can be no separateness in something that is not a thing. Only the human bodies are separate from each other, but you were here before your body came.

Take a moment to read through that list and confirm it inside yourself. Check again that you are not actually a "someone" at all but the "no-thing-ness".

We can look at this revelation and begin to see that if we do not need anything at all on our highest level, then we can begin to allow that realisation to permeate our world. Once you know with conviction and clarity that you are all that you already need, it begins to transform all our relationships. Most of us interact with each other from a place of need even if we do not realise it. We are unconsciously looking for what we think we need from others, because we do not realise we already have it within. As the realisation deepens that you are not separate from anything, you will be able to experience much more happiness, peace and an absence of conflict inside yourself.

Exercises for Stage Five

1. Look back at your list from stage one and identify what you feel you are separate from in each one. Are you separating yourself from your mother, father, sister, from money or time? Have a look in detail and see that you cannot in fact be separate from it.

2. For each item on the list see if you can identify what you feel you really want. As we imagine we are separate we believe deeply that we are going to die and that we are vulnerable. Most of us move around in the world looking for security, acceptance, respect, time, abundance and more. For example if you want more money from your boss at work, you can see you might feel that money will bring greater freedom and security. If you want more respect from your partner, you might see that what you actually want is greater self-respect.

3. For each thing that you think you need, whether it is a tangible thing or intangible, accept that it must already be present within you because you are all of life and its source too. If it is already present within

you then you can begin to allow it to show itself rather than seeking it from an external source. Perhaps you may also be able to see that you were bound to fail to get what you want when you are trying to get based on the false idea that you are separate and need to get it from "out there".

4. Recognise that there is no "out there". It is all you.

The impact of this stage may take some time to fully digest but you will begin to see immediate results in the way you feel and how other people treat you. You will also find that all the actions you were taking to get what you want are much more effective now that your energy is flowing stronger and you are clearer on what you actually are.

CHAPTER II

Transcending the Vasanas Course Lesson Four

Stage Six

Introduction

This final stage will help you to firmly and totally understand the previous one and it will also expand it further for you. It may seem very spiritual and specific but we must remember that all our vasanas are manifesting on all levels. This stage will focus on healing the spiritual level of our being. There are a few core false beliefs that keep this layer of being suffering and we will begin to undo them here.

Stage Six — The belief in otherness

In this stage we are going to look deeper into what it means to be formless. We may have used self-inquiry to effectively eliminate any tendencies to think of ourselves still as a thing, an object or something perceivable. We may have come to understand that we are formless and beyond being damaged, ageless and timeless; but we may not have realised the full implications of what it means to be formless. We can still hold other people, events and things we seem to need as being "other" than us. For this stage of the process to be fully understood and assimilated, we must come to see that there is nothing other than us. If you are formless and cannot find an end to yourself when you look, then you must be all that exists. You are the emptiness or nothingness from which all forms arise and are made out of.

At this point I could instruct you to stop and deeply contemplate this and you should; however this would not eliminate what will happen in this next stage. Let us look closer at what is next in this disassembly process that we are applying to each vasana and see if we can understand why.

You are the source of all that exists and you are all that ever has existed, exists right now and could exist in the future. What you are is the formlessness which contains all possibilities of what may manifest and all that has manifested into actuality.

As you read and apply and comprehend this, you will come to feel a deep sense of peace, completion and as if you are living in a place that is involved in the world of people, events and things but is also somehow protected and immune to the dramas of the world. Every once in a while, you will come across something that seems to make you suffer again but this is not what is actually happening.

It is important that you take a moment to read and fully contemplate the following statement:

Each time you feel you are suffering again you must look and find out what is being shown to you. Life is trying to show you what you have left out of your Allness. You are all of the un-manifest formlessness and the manifest too. If there is anything you have left out of that, then you will feel a sense of division inside yourself because there will seem to be "me and other".

What you really want is to feel better and to live without conflict inside yourself. You are the unmanifest source of all which has no vibration and also the manifest which is vibrating. If there is a difference between the vibration of what we are actually living and what we would like then we will feel this as a sense of discord or conflict in our energy. We can describe it many ways but it's just energy that isn't flowing as well as it could because some ideas that we have are getting in the way. When we believe these ideas we do not allow our energy to flow and manifest as it wants to.

Naturally we are happy, peaceful and abundant beings but most of us have cut off that flow of energy so much by believing we are separate beings that we suffer mentally, emotionally and physically most of the time. What we really want is to realise our Oneness with all of life and to live fully from that place. Our life can become an ever-expansive and more abundant journey where there is no fear at all. The source of fear is the belief that there is "other" than me; that other things exist except me.

We may have seen deeply in the last stage that you are not separate but we may not have come to completely understand the implications of that. In this stage, we will come to see that we have always been the One Being manifesting as many animate beings and inanimate objects. There is not a single thing that has existed or ever will, that is not you appearing as something else. Once you begin to realise this you will radiate love to the world and to each person you meet. This is not a personal love but an impersonal and unconditional acceptance of the person as they are.

What you really want is to have no resistance in your energy, to be without conflict and to do this, we have to realise the idea there is "other" than me is not true.

To do this let's take a look at the false belief in this stage:

- **I am formless but other people, places, events and things are still real and separate, there is an end to my formlessness. Everything else is "other" than me.**
- **The manifest is different to the un-manifest and I am un-manifest. The manifest forms in the universe are "other" than me.**

These beliefs are so pervasive in our consciousness that we do not even begin to question them unless we begin to suffer. We can see that they are also completely accepted as true by society, so much so that it seems strange to most people why we would even question what we are. The idea of "me" being separate automatically comes with the idea of "otherness" built into it.

If we study our evolution as human beings, we can see that the left brain is responsible for this feeling of being separate. This side of our brain is the more analytical side and is used for quantifying differences between things. The left brain evolved from a primitive animal brain that had to judge quickly if something was a threat, food or a potential mate. As such this side of our brain became very good at recognising things based on their colour, size, shape and other characteristics. It gathers data about our world and stores it as a frame of reference. To do this it has to judge the difference between two objects and so the idea of "me" and "other than me" was born.

The right side of the human brain is able to see Oneness, that all is included in the Self that we are, the formless nature of our true self is evident from here. In the highest human evolution we can learn to function from both sides of the brain, to appreciate the differing and unique ways that the One Being is manifesting in its infinite diversity and yet to know beyond doubt that there is no separation in reality and that it only seems that way. From here, we can begin to live our highest human experience as the Conscious Being recognising itself wherever it looks.

To live from this advanced state of consciousness, we must begin to see where we are still seeing a separation between things. At this stage the idea of "other" can be hiding subtly so it is important to look carefully throughout your life. If we are not separate then we are ALL of this manifest and unmanifest. We are the Allness and nothing can be left out of Allness or else it is not Allness anymore by definition.

We will look at an example to help illustrate this point before moving on to the exercises for this stage.

Example 1 — Jenny had wanted a promotion from her boss to get more recognition of her efforts, more money and a greater level of challenge in her job. Over the years, she has been at this current job she has seen a few people promoted before her and this has been a recurring pattern.

She had asked for a reason why she wasn't being promoted and never got a straight answer. Jenny had even applied for another job in a different company out of frustration but didn't get it.

Throughout this process of transcending the vasanas, Jenny had come to see that she was hoping her outer actions would fix this problem but that was not true. She saw it was her inner anger at her boss and other work colleagues, her frustration and sense of injustice that was the issue. Jenny recognised she had not been allowing the emotions to be felt and so she allowed each emotion as it came as fully as she could.

When the same feelings came up again, Jenny recognised that she must have some root belief deep down that was holding all this in place and so she contemplated and saw she really felt that she was not good enough to deserve a better job. This was quite shocking to Jenny but she felt she transcended the vasana and had a shift in her level of consciousness.

Jenny felt frustrated again when the same pattern came back, until she remembered it was because it was ready to be taken to the next stage. She looked deeply at what she was and saw she was not actually a person who was alone in the world, separated from everyone else. She could see this idea of separation was not true and therefore she could not want or need a better job. The question of her worthiness also seemed to vanish as she looked deeper into it.

Finally Jenny noticed the same pattern once again and began to look at why. Jenny contemplated for quite some time and asked herself "what am I leaving out of my Allness?" She was startled to see she still saw her boss as separate and the money she wanted to earn. She still felt that the respect and recognition she had wanted was "out there" and that she had to get it. After contemplating deeply on this, she realised all was within her and she was at peace. Out of the blue another company offered Jenny her dream job and she took it. She now feels happier than ever and able to see all the employees at her work as a part of herself.

Exercises for Stage Six

1. For each item on your list from stage one, identify all the things you may have still felt a subtle sense of

separation from. Start with the easier tangible things, such as your wife, husband, child or friend.

2. On the next level identify any things that you are trying to get and therefore holding as other than you. Many of these things might be much more subtle though and hard to identify. Examples of these might be money, time, friendship, respect, justice or anything at all that you seem to need more of, less of or to come to peace with. Anything that you have a relationship with is seen as other than you. What do I mean by relationship? I mean that you have to do something with it, get it, get rid of it or do anything at all with it.

3. Next look at the extremely subtle things you are still separating yourself from. Examples of these could be emotional feelings you are wanting or even states of awareness you are chasing. It may be peace, love, joy, satisfaction or any other similar item that you are wanting or needing. To completely transcend the vasana so that it will not return again, you must come to see that you cannot be separate from even these things. They must be present here already even if only in potential, waiting to become an actual reality. They are all happening inside you, manifesting in you and disappearing in you. By including everything in your Allness, you will feel a deep peace, satisfaction and happiness that nothing in the world can disturb.

Please note, this last stage can challenge you to see the subtle nature of the things you are still holding as separate or other than you. Most spiritual seekers will have identified they are not separate to other human beings but will still hold a level of consciousness they wish to achieve or a state of bliss as "out there" or still to be achieved. Ask for help if you need to, I am here for you. The more you wish to see yourself in your Allness the happier your

life will be because there will be no "other" to disturb you. This leads to a total absence of fear.

SECTION THREE

CHAPTER 12

The Abundance, Manifestation and Desire Course

Introduction

This course is designed to clarify exactly what abundance is and how it is already showing itself to you. Many of us have been taught to feel that abundance is something we must get and learn to receive but we will challenge that deeply. How can you learn to receive something that is already here and omnipresent? It would be like me asking you to learn to receive the oxygen in the air; you don't need to, you are surrounded by it.

We will also take a look at how the un-manifest becomes the manifest and learn some vital information about this process. Once we understand how things come from the un-manifest infinite potentiality, through subtle forms and into more tangible forms, we will then be in a position to recognise clearly how we are creating the outer world we see. Most of us have been creating what we don't want accidentally, over and over. Through this course, we will learn how to understand key aspects of the manifestation process and use them for the things we want right now.

Finally, we will update our understanding of desire and how to use it to make sure we are on course to see abundance showing up in the ways that make us happy and satisfied. Some spiritual teachings can leave us feeling as if we have done something wrong if we still have desires for things. Desire is not wrong and we all have desires for things. Even the wish to achieve Self-Realisation is still a desire and we all desire to take another breath after this one!

The more we can understand why we want what we want, then we will find those desires appearing faster and more easily. We will look at how to transcend programming that we all have that makes us feel deep down that we don't deserve to get what we want and that we can't get what we want unless we work hard. One of the ways we limit ourselves is by believing things simply cannot come to us effortlessly and joyfully.

CHAPTER 13

Abundance, Manifestation and Desire Course Lesson One
There Is No Lack

Introduction

In this lesson we are going to be looking at what abundance actually is, as opposed to what we think it is. We will reveal a few basic ideas that we might be believing that make it very challenging for us to experience the fullness of life. Some of these ideas will be so believed by us that it may seem ridiculous to even question their truth, especially if we seem to keep experiencing them as true. We will start from the basics and build until we are in a position to expose these beliefs and see that they cannot be true. I would urge you to confirm what you read in each lesson and make it your own experiential truth.

What are you?

We must begin this course by taking an open look at what you really are. Only once you have an understanding of your real nature will it become easier to see what abundance is and why it has to show up for you.

Take a look at what you are right now as you read this. Take a moment and scan yourself and see what you find. You will find a human body of course and you will find a mind with thoughts. You may also notice emotions and sensations within your body such as pain, tension, discomfort or pleasurable sensations. All of these you say are "my" or "mine"; notice you would say "my body" and not "me". You would probably say "my mind is driving me crazy" or "my emotions are all over the place today". We know all about the "my" and "mine" but what are you actually?

If you look right now for this "me" or "I" you will not find anything concrete, only a vague sense that you are here. If you continue to look you will see that what you really are is not a thing at all, you are not an object. The idea that you are a "someone" is not quite true when we really look. We can come to see that what we are has no form and is not solid. Your body, thoughts and emotions are things that you can see inside you but yourself you cannot see.

At first this can be a little disturbing to realise but if you allow yourself time to be with this realisation you will begin to find it brings peace and a sense of wellbeing. If you are not a thing then you cannot be hurt or killed and you cannot die. You are unmanifest in your purest form and all manifest things emerge out of you.

Manifestation occurs out of you and you are the source of all things.

The Manifestation Process

The unmanifest you, the not-a-thing-yet-ness that you are, is like a field of infinite possibilities. Imagine that all possibilities for anything that can exist at all is present inside you, you have infinite power. The manifestation process occurs gradually and moves from subtle forms of being into more and more tangible forms. At first things move from the un-manifest into the manifest as a thought form, an idea that comes and gathers more and more momentum. Then it solidifies even more as a feeling, an emotion and finally into a physical thing that you can see, feel or experience in the world around you.

Manifestation always occurs at 100% of what is possible. Manifestation always occurs as the highest possibility that is available and being allowed in any moment. This means we are always experiencing the manifestation of something and we cannot turn off things becoming manifest. Things cannot halfway manifest and stop. They cannot also manifest at half power. The unmanifest is always completely manifesting.

I will try to explain this with a metaphor. If we take a glass of water that has just boiled, we will see steam rising from the water. We can say that the water represents the unmanifest you and the steam represents the manifest aspect of you.

Notice the following:

- The steam is not only half rising, it is steaming as much as it possibly can in each moment. The unmanifest Self that you are is completely manifesting as much as it can in any moment as something. There can be no absence of manifesting, no moment where nothing appears.
- The steam cannot stop rising on its own as it has no power, its power comes from the hot water. The manifest has no power of its own because it is only an appearance of things; it is the pure unmanifest potential "condensed down" and so it would be like trying to tell the steam to stop rising. You could only stop that by doing something to the hot water.
- The size and shape of the steam is always moving and changing yet the hot water remains unchanged. This is a metaphor for how the unmanifest you is always the same and the manifest aspect of you (your body, thoughts, emotions, life and world) is always changing and in constant motion.
- The steam and the water are the same but they appear to be different. The manifest looks different to the unmanifest you, which is invisible and formless but they are the same thing, they are One.

Consider this deeply and you will come to see there is no lack. We are raised to believe that there can be a void or absence of manifestation, a hole in infinity where "nothing showed up" but we must come to see that the unmanifest is always showing up as something, just as the water can only steam at 100%. Even if the unmanifest is "only" showing up as empty space, it MUST be appearing as something because that is all it can do.

Now of course there are many times in our life where we seem to lack what we want and we might feel inclined to say that what we want is absent and we are experiencing the lack of it. In truth we must admit that what we don't want is showing up in abundance. There has to be an abundance of something and what we focus on will increase and expand.

To be able to see that the unmanifest MUST show up as something manifest allows us to begin to move beyond the major obstacle to abundance in all its forms. We can begin to see that there can be no lack or "not-enough-ness" at all. It is like the manifestation process is stuck at the "on" switch and cannot be switched off. Once we see this, we can know that we have been creating something with our beliefs, desires and allowing or resisting it and we can come to use this process consciously to create what we DO want to have.

The Observer Effect

Let's now look at a little science to help us begin to see how we have been shaping what has been showing up for us and why. Don't worry, you can still apply this process and make abundance show up for you in a way you will love. You do not even need to understand this section. In fact most of us can skip this section altogether and it won't make a difference. I only include it for those (like myself) who like proof of how it happens and why something is occurring to help let go of resistance to it.

The Observer Effect states that the simple fact of observing something makes it change and behave differently than it would if we did not observe it. The more we observe it, the more we affect its manifestation endpoint into physicality. In simple human terms, it means that whatever we are focusing our attention on, we will get more of because our expectation allows a certain thing to manifest.

What science hasn't proved as yet is as the level of consciousness of the observer increases, so does the effect you have on what is manifesting. What does this mean for us? It means we cannot focus on anything for too long without it showing up again and again and the further along the spiritual path we are, the greater the effect.

The vicious circle of belief, expectation and manifestation

What has already manifested also affects what will manifest in the future. This means if we see the appearance of lack all around us, we will be focused on and expecting more lack. Therefore, it has no option but to come to us in the same way.

We must be sure to focus on what we want only and not on what we don't want. This is why we need to know that there is no lack possible and so we must be getting what we have put our attention upon. We must know that abundance must appear in some form and it is up to us to mould it consciously and shape it. We have all been doing that unconsciously and accidentally.

The first thing that happens when we want something is the opposite of it, or appearance of lack of it, shows up. This is so we can know that it must be here, right now in some way. We must come to trust that what we want is here in some less tangible form, rather than believing our mind which will be telling us it is not here at all.

Summary of the manifestation process

Unmanifest → desire and attention → thought form/idea → attention → emotional result → attention → physical manifestation

Most of us are using this process unconsciously and keep creating what we don't want. We believe that we can be denied what we want and so we keep creating what we don't want by default and noticing it. We observe what we don't want and put attention on it and then we get more of it.

This is what is happening in our experience for most of us:

Physical manifestation of what we don't want → attention on what we don't want → negative thoughts about what we want → negative emotions → more physical manifestation of what we don't want.

And so the cycle goes on and it reinforces the belief that we cannot have what we want. It may also perpetuate feelings of unworthiness, as we may begin to feel we are not good enough and cannot have what we desire. If we can come to see that we are always getting an abundance of something then this lesson has been successful. ☺

Exercises for Lesson One

Have a look at your life and see if you can begin to identify where you may have been using this process unconsciously and getting what you don't want. You might want to include the following areas:

- Career or life purpose
- Finances
- Romance or marriage
- Family
- Friendships and other relationships
- Spiritual Pathway
- Health

And any other areas you can think of. You do not have to share this list with anyone and I would urge you not to blame yourself for anything that you have accidentally created. You could not use this process consciously whilst you still believed in lack and that it was possible for the absence to exist. Now that you know this, you can forgive yourself and allow abundance to show up for you in ways that will make you feel good and happy.

CHAPTER 14

Abundance, Manifestation and Desire Course Lesson Two

Desire is How the Manifest Universe Expands

Introduction

In this lesson we will be looking at the subject of desire and how to work with it. Many spiritual and religious teachings can leave us with the sense that we should have no desire or that we should be able to transcend it. We will look at the effect this has had on our consciousness and once and for all clarify what desire is and how it can help you.

Desire is life trying to expand.

It is natural that we will feel desire many times in our day. The desire to survive and continue existing is the most basic of all desires and fuels many others. We all have the desire to find a mate, get the perfect job, to have a family or even to have an awakening in our consciousness. We must come to see that desire is not wrong and we are supposed to have it. Even a desire to take another breath after this one is a desire and it is one worth having!

In lesson one we came to see that we are the unmanifest and the manifest Self and that the manifest is always moving and changing. The whole of manifestation as we know it is the universe and scientists have concluded that it is expanding and this is true of us too. We will always have this desire for "more". Whatever we want out of life we must come to see that it is our nature to expand. We are life (the manifest world) and we are also the source of all life (the unmanifest) and each experience we have will leave us wanting more. We can feel sometimes that we are hungry for a bigger and better experience of life and we feel it through our personal desires. We are not a separate person at all but when life wants to expand we will feel it in our bodies as "I want".

We will begin to find that even though it feels as if there is a separate person called "me" that has a desire, it is really life that is expanding. There is nothing wrong with feeling a want, wish or desire and we will look at how we can work with this energy of desire and to stop resisting it. Many of us who are on spiritual pathways can feel that we are wrong to have desires and that we should get rid of them or ignore them. Like anything else that we push away, desire will only grow more in our experience. The more things that we want but don't allow to come to us, the more we will find ourselves wanting. The universe is "hearing" our energetic vibration and if we resist desire, we will find that we are saying "I want" which is the same as "I don't have". When this occurs, we can find ourselves in a never-ending loop of wanting something that never seems to arrive.

How desire helps things to manifest

You may recall from lesson one that things come into a physical reality in a very subtle manifest level to a more and more tangible form. Anything that we want will arise first from the unmanifest at the level of thought. This is a desire or wish that we notice as the sense "I want" or "I would like" or a general urge for more of something.

Next it will move to manifest in a more tangible way and we will feel a sense of it becoming closer and we will have an emotional response. Finally we will notice the thing that we want actually appearing as a physical object in our life. If it was a feeling that we have been desiring, such as more respect from others, we will notice people coming into our life and events happening that leave us feeling more respected.

The more that we want something, the faster it will appear in our reality because we are putting a lot of attention, energy and time on the things that we want. When we want something very badly, we focus on it a lot and will have a lot of thoughts about it, we will also feel very strong emotions about it too. It will then show up physically in our life.

How to decode our desires

All of us have had experiences of wanting something and it came to us easily and also we have all had the opposite experience. We can all probably think of things that we wanted that simply did not arrive. We can begin to look deeper at our desires to find out why the manifestation process did not go as we wished. Here are some reasons to consider:

1. We don't believe that we can get what we want, so it has to not show up to fulfil our expectations.
2. We have some unconscious beliefs that will be violated if we get what we want and so it cannot happen for us.
3. We are focused more on what we DON'T want than what we want and so we must keep watching it play out again and again.
4. We don't really want the thing we are thinking about, we are unconsciously associating it with something else (i.e. we may think we want money but we don't really want that; we want the happiness we think money will give us).
5. What we think we want is only an outer expression of the real thing we want (i.e. we may think we want a romantic relationship when what we actually want is the feeling of security and intimacy that would bring us).

In this lesson we are going to look at numbers 4 and 5 and learn how to find out what we really want. Most of us have no clear idea of what we want and even if we do, we may not know why we want it. These facts are good to know because we can save ourselves a lot of time, energy and heartbreak when we find out what we actually want and why.

Questions

We can use some simple questions to find out what we really want. It is worth asking yourself:

- What do I really want?
- Why do I want it?
- What will happen if I don't get it?

Using these simple questions can help us to get to the root desire and manifest it faster. The questions can also help us to see if we are hoping that getting what we want will make us feel a certain way. We will look at two examples of conversations I have had with students to help us understand this point.

Example 1

Student — I want more money in my life, there just never seems to be enough.

Me — Why do you want that?

S — Well, I want to be able to pay my bills easily each month and have some spare to do what I want.

Me — So what you really want is to be able to do more things you want to.

S — Well, yes I guess so.

Me — And why do you want that?

S — Well, it will be more fun and I will be able to treat the kids more.

Me — So what you really want is to treat your kids and have fun right?

S — Wow yes I never saw it that way but yes.

Me — Why do you want to treat your kids more?

S — Because I want to feel like a good mum and I want them to know I love them.

Me — And why do you want that?

S — (After long pause) Because I will feel better, I will feel good.

Me — So after all that, can you see that what you really want is to feel good? Try to hold that as your main desire and see what happens. Let the universe decide how to bring you situations, people and events that will make you feel good.

See if you can trust that it will also involve more money, happier kids and all the things you thought you wanted.

S — Ok I will do that thanks!

In this example, we can see that the student was asking really to feel good but insisting that it comes only through getting more money without realising. Once we got to the root of the desire and the student focused on feeling good, she found life began to bring her many surprising ways to feel good and these were more delightful than anything she could have designed in her own mind.

Example 2

Student — I really wish my brother and sister would stop fighting. They always put me in the middle and I have to sort it out for them when they won't talk to each other.

Me — So why do you want them to stop fighting?

S — Because I don't want to be in the middle of it anymore.

Me — Why do you want that?

S — Sometimes I feel like they just want me there to help sort out their issues and they don't really value spending time with me.

Me — Can you see that what you really want is for your brother and sister to enjoy your company just for who you are and that they want to be with you.

S — Yes, I can see that.

Me — And what will happen if you don't get them to like being with you?

S — I guess I will feel that they don't like me.

Me — And what happens if they don't like you enough?

S — I will feel like I am not a good enough sister to them.

Me — And what will happen then?

S — I will feel bad.

Me — So what you really want is to feel good.

In this example, we can see that what this woman really wanted was to feel good about herself and that she was a good sister to her siblings. She had almost made it impossible for herself to feel good though because she was really saying to herself "I can only be happy if my brother and sister stop fighting amongst themselves". This is something that she has very little, if any, control over and so she was stuck in a negative feedback loop.

After some time, she came to see this and began to focus on feeling happy. Even when she was sometimes in the middle of her siblings again, she felt much better in knowing there really was nothing she could nor needed to do. She saw that it was up to them to work it through and it need not make her doubt her self-worth just because she could not stop them arguing.

Exercises for Lesson Two

1. Spend some time thinking about the main things you want from life. These desires could be material things such as cars, money, a husband or more subtle things like wanting more time, happiness or even peace. You might want to use your answers from lesson one exercises to help you with this.

2. For each of your desires ask yourself why you want it. Keep going with this "why" question as far as you can. If you feel stuck or unable to get an answer, you can then ask "what happens if I do not get this?"

3. See if you can notice how you have been expecting people, events and situations to give you good feelings, when what you really want is to feel good. Make a promise to yourself if you can, that the most important thing is that you value how you feel first. This will bring the things into your life that you want. It is the more direct route to get what you want.

CHAPTER 15

Abundance, Manifestation and Desire Course Lesson Three
Learning to Allow

Introduction

In lesson one we began to understand that something IS going to manifest and that there cannot be a void in our reality. Next, we learnt that it is our desire that is shaping and moulding what shows up in physical form. In this lesson we are going to look at how to allow what you want to come to you. Each time we desire something it is given to us but we must learn how to hold the right vibration long enough for it to make it all the way through the manifestation levels.

Manifestation Process

At first everything that could manifest is present as potential only, it is a possibility in the unmanifest Self that we are and it is not actually anything as yet. As we experience something that we do not want, or something that is unsatisfactory about our life, our manifestation process begins in the form of a desire. Desire is really a thought that says "I want" or "I don't want". As we continue to hold this idea of what we want, we gather more like-minded thoughts around it.

The next stage of our manifestation process is an emotional manifestation. This is in the form of an emotional feeling about what we want. Emotions are slower and lower vibrations than thoughts. Our desire is "condensing" down from pure potential (that has no vibration), to a thought form which is vibrating very fast and into an emotional feeling.

Next is the physical manifestation, as the thing we have wanted appears in some form in our experience. If we have been holding an allowing vibration, we will see the thing become physically manifest in our experience and we will have felt positive emotions. These positive emotions are vibrations being felt and they will condense even more into a physical object if we allow that to occur.

We will now take a look at the three main reasons we do not get what we want every time:

Reason Number 1: We don't believe we can get it.

Reason Number 2: We have a negative belief about the thing we want, about ourselves or anything else and as such we feel negative emotions and cannot allow it to physically manifest. What WILL manifest is more of what we don't want!

Reason Number 3: We have got into a habit of noticing what we don't want and keep perpetuating that cycle unintentionally.

These reasons make us feel negative emotions when we think about what we want. A negative emotion means we are vibrating on a frequency that is too low and slow to allow the thing we want to materialise. A positive emotion means we are vibrating on a level that is allowing this "condensing" process to occur.

Allowing our manifestation to materialise

Our manifest nature is always vibrating and we know that our thoughts, feelings and every atom of our body is also vibrating. To allow something to manifest in the way we want physically, we must ensure that we maintain a similar vibration to how we feel when we think about what it would be like to have it already.

If we can slow things right down and look at what happens when we get something we want, we will see that we begin to feel good, or to feel better than we did before. If we look even closer, we will see that the "I want" feeling makes us feel bad emotionally because we believe we do not have it as yet. When the thing we want shows up in our life in a physical form, the feeling of "I want" goes away and is replaced by "I have". This is why we begin to feel better.

In lesson two we looked at why we wanted the things we want. We saw that in many cases we want them because we want to feel good or better than we do right now. If we can look intelligently at this process, we will see that most of us are doing this backwards. We want something because we think it will make us feel good when we get it but because we don't feel we have it yet, we are feeling bad and not allowing it.

A major leap in our level of consciousness comes when we begin to see that it MUST already be here in some form. Once you can no longer believe the thought "I don't have it yet", then you will find it very hard to feel negative emotion about it and it will show up in a physical way as quickly as possible.

Once we realise that what we want is already here on a thought level AND an emotional level, we will begin to feel good. By the laws of creation it must then come in a physical form too. We must be mature enough to know that it is already present and dis-believe any idea that it is not. We can begin to ask intelligent questions such as "in what way it is already here?" or "On what level have I been dis-allowing it?"

We must begin to see the evidence that we are feeling better and better about what we want each day as our measure of success. As humans we are taught to ONLY value what we want once it shows up for us in a physical way and we disregard completely the emotional and mental aspect of the manifestation process. If we can begin to value our improving emotional state as evidence of our success then we will allow everything to come into physical form too.

When we judge our success by whether or not it has shown up physically yet, we are bound to continue to perpetuate this cycle of not getting what we want. When can begin to see emotional success and a feeling of wellbeing as a precursor for the physical manifestation, we will be able to allow the process to come to fruition.

Specific and non-specific desires

When we begin to see and accept that everything we desire is desired because we believe it will make us feel better once we receive it, we can begin to turn the process around and work in a much smarter way. Instead of asking for a specific thing, we can begin to ask for an emotional state or spiritual realisation. In doing so, our desires become less specific and we will receive what we want much faster and there will be less resistance to the process.

When we ask for a feeling or emotional state as our required outcome, we will receive this much faster AND also a host of physical manifestations that help us to feel the way we want to feel. A general desire is more easily identified and allowed than waiting for one specific physical object to help us feel the way we want for a short time.

We will now look at a few examples of specific desires and then turn them into more general desires that can manifest more easily:

Example 1: "I want a better job so I can get more money. I want to pay off my debts but I don't have the spare money right now. I get frustrated that I can't make it happen faster."

This is a very specific desire at the moment but if we were to ask why this person wants this we might find the following desire is really underneath it all as is much more general:

"Why do I want this? Well I want to have financial freedom, the ability to do what I want, when I want and not have to work all the time."

So we can see that the real desire underneath wanting a better job is a desire for financial freedom. Again, we can ask why this person wants that:

"I want financial freedom because I don't want any worries. I want to feel free and be spontaneous whenever I want. I don't want to be limited".

So we can see the root of all this is a desire for feeling free and unlimited. If we can focus our attention on that only, we will find life giving us all kinds of physical ways that make us feel that way.

When we insist on our desire being specific, we are limiting the universe to how it can come and saying it must be only through this one avenue and no other way.

Example 2: "I want a better relationship, my current partner doesn't treat me with respect and isn't romantic. I want to meet someone new who is nicer".

We can distil this desire down to its more general nature by realising that what this person actually wants is to feel loved, valued and respected. When we keep our desire at this general level, we will find all kinds of things begin to happen to make us feel this way including, but not limited to, a romantic relationship.

Spiritual transcendence of desire

We can manifest our desires much faster if we can begin to see that our desires are morphing into a sense that we already have what we want. We will find that the sense "I want" or "I need" is noticed as it arises and then we will be able to define it more generally to help speed the manifestation process.

Ultimately, what will allow your desire to manifest in the easiest and fastest way is to acknowledge your "I want" feeling totally but to then let it transcend this level to become a feeling of "I already have". We can know from lesson one that it must already be here on a thought level and that we already have what we desire as a thought form.

We can further transcend now, by noticing with our more general desires we are allowing it to be here already on an emotional level. So we can feel it is true when we say "I already have it on 2 of the 3 levels and I am excited to see how it shows up physically".

I want to state again clearly that there is nothing wrong with having desires. I am simply stating that to allow the desire to turn into a feeling of already having what we want is the fastest way to allow what we want to materialise.

Simply put, the more we feel good emotionally, the easier it is to allow things to come to us to make us feel even better. This is a much easier process than insisting that one particular thing, such as a job or relationship, makes us feel good because if it does not appear for us we will feel bad. This will keep us in a negative feedback loop of seeing what we don't want, feeling bad about it and therefore getting more of what we don't want.

The better way is to desire to feel good and then as we do we will see the physical evidence of that showing up for us, which will allow us to feel even better. We will be in a positive feedback loop of "the better I feel, the better it gets!"

"I need" is realised to be "I want". Then, "I want" becomes "I have already" and then the ultimate is "I am".

Exercises for Lesson Three

- Take a look at your answers for lesson one and two exercises and see if you can write down a list of more general desires. These will appear more in the form of emotional states that you want or success in a particular area of life.
- Recognise that for each one you are not discounting what you wanted in lesson one exercises but you are simply using a much more efficient way to get it.

CHAPTER 16

Abundance, Manifestation and
Desire Course Lesson Four
Letting Go of Resistance

Introduction

In this last lesson of the course, we will look at the reasons why we do not always allow what we want to come to us. The manifestation process has been described before but we will remind ourselves of it now to help it be understood better. Our consciousness learns by receiving new information several times until it becomes familiar, at which point it is absorbed and acted upon.

The Manifestation Process is as follows:

1. At first, there is only the Infinite Unmanifest field of potentialities.
2. Then, due to contrast (we experience what we don't want) a desire is born as a thought form.

3. Next, the desire gathers momentum attracting similar frequency thoughts.
4. Then, the desire manifests on the emotional level and we will feel good when we think about it.
5. Finally, if we can hold an emotionally good feeling long enough the desire will manifest on the physical level either as the thing we wanted or something that will make us feel just as good or better.

So what is the reason it sometimes takes a lot longer than we want it to? And why do we sometimes feel negative emotions about what we want? The reason for the way we feel is that we have resistance to what we want and to the process of our evolution.

What is resistance and why do we have it?

All of us have some beliefs that lie deep within our consciousness, that have been there through many lifetimes and that are the cause of our challenges and negative karma. We are also programmed with beliefs by the adults that took care of us as infants — of course the adults did not do this on purpose. Most of us have no choice but to pass along these beliefs to those around us, and our children. This programming is also added to by social peer groups, the media and many forms of advertising, religious dogma, political agendas and more.

As we grow and pick up these beliefs about ourselves, we have no skills with which to investigate if they are true or not, so the only option we have is to suppress the emotional response to them. Also, as children we do not usually even feel it is right to question these beliefs if they have come from a trusted authority figure. Beliefs such as "I am not good enough" or "I am not safe" are so painful to us that we bury them deep down under layers of thoughts so that we do not even remember they are there.

In our innocence we have no choice but to accept these beliefs as our consciousness takes on any information that we receive on faith that it is correct. Simply put, it does not even occur to us that it might not be true. Once we have accepted these beliefs to be true, we must then find evidence that they are true by manifesting more of what we do not want. By the time we come to try to consciously use this process and to manifest what we do want, we may have had many years of proving to ourselves unconsciously that we are in fact not good enough to have what we want and that we do not deserve to be happy.

This may sound quite extreme but every person has some amount of this programming. Whilst this programming remains mostly unconscious to us, we are unable to look at the beliefs and re-examine them to see if they are actually true. Our mind assumes again and again that they are true and until we can bring them into our conscious awareness, we will be trapped in the cycle, bound to repeat the same pattern over and over. We must consciously choose to look at this programming from our new place of maturity. In this lesson we will learn how to expose these beliefs and move beyond their effect, once and for all.

Whilst we do not know we have the belief within us we have no choice but to keep believing it on a deep level. Once we see it consciously we can realise it is not true and move beyond it. Only then can we get what we want.

The process of releasing resistance

We may not be conscious of which beliefs are operating within us but we can allow our emotions to let us know when they are operating. If we can learn to pay attention to how we feel emotionally, then we can see when a belief is operating and sabotaging our ability to manifest our desires. The first thing to do when we feel a negative emotion is to soften any resistance to looking at it and what may be causing it. We are all programmed to want to avoid looking at things that make us feel bad but once we are conscious of this, then we can move beyond it.

We feel a negative emotion because we are believing some negative thoughts but are not conscious of what they are. We can invite the emotion to tell us what the belief is that is causing it, by wanting to see it. We feel negative emotions during the manifestation process, usually because we do not feel that we can have what we want but we are not as yet aware of that.

First, we must bring awareness of the thoughts that are causing the emotion and not allowing manifestation to show up as we want. We do this by being willing to see it, then sustaining our attention on it long enough for it to be transcended.

We do not have to do anything to transcend a negative belief. It will go on its own once we see it and accept fully it is there. Bringing it into the light of our conscious attention is enough. The reason that we do not do this very often as human beings is because we believe that to look at these ideas we have about ourselves, will be overwhelmingly painful and difficult and it will leave us feeling broken and lost. In fact, the reverse is true and the more we look at a negative belief in a safe way, the more empowered we will feel. We will finally be able to transcend the belief and not be at the effect of it.

The statement process

The statement process is a simple and safe way to look at any emotion, belief or resistance that we may be having and to unravel it in an empowering way.

There are two main steps to the statement process and they are easy to learn:

1. We write down a statement that feels true to us right now about the situation. There may be a lot of negative emotion about it as we write it.

2. Next, we write a statement that also feels true right now, that is in no way denying the situation, but that feels just a little better right now.

The rules are easy for this process, we simply continue to write a series of statements and each one must feel true right now and is softening the resistance a little each time. Sometimes you can feel a tension in your body if a negative belief is playing, or it may feel like angst, fear, anger or any negative emotional state. We are simply looking for a statement that feels true AND feels a little better than the previous one. We may notice this as a sense of relief in the body, a sense of lightening or relaxation or a lessening of the negative emotion.

In the statement process we are NOT looking to resolve the issue you are writing about, we are simply looking to feel a little bit better about it in a step-by-step way. Everyone can do this once they get used to how it works.

Theoretically, we should all just be able to stop focusing on what we don't want to manifest and start focusing on what we DO want to show up. This can be very difficult when we are in the habit of noticing what we don't want and it is showing up in abundance.

If we need more money right now because we cannot pay our bills, we will find that to simply think, write or try to believe "I am financially free and all my bills are paid easily", will actually make us feel WORSE because it seems so very untrue to us right now. Yes, it is where we want to be eventually but the truth of it is that right now we do not believe that it will happen for us. No amount of positive thinking or affirming what we do want will help at this point and it may only make it worse because it feels so untrue. Positive thinking, or affirmations, can remind us that we have so far failed to make this manifestation process work in a way we want. They will only add to the belief that we are somehow not good enough because we cannot figure this out.

We will go through our examples again from lesson three and use the statement process to work our way back to feeling good about it again:

Example 1. "I want a better job so I can get more money. I want to pay off my debts but I don't have the spare money right now. I get frustrated that I can't make it happen faster."

So this statement can be our first statement, it feels very true right now and it is describing the situation. Next we will look for something we can write that feels true and just a little bit better than that:

1. I want a better job so I can get more money. I want to pay off my debts but I don't have the spare money right now. I get frustrated that I can't make it happen faster.
2. Perhaps if I get a little extra money I can begin to pay off one of my debts. Even paying off one is better than none.

3. I know as I pay off one debt, I will have more spare money to put into paying off the next one.

4. I can see I will be saving money as the interest won't be piling up so much.

5. Maybe I will get a better job at some point too and that will help.

6. Many people I know live with debts and don't get so frustrated with them.

7. Maybe I can come to feel more comfortable with them over time.

8. I think I might be feeling that I cannot be successful until I am debt-free.

9. Yes, I can see that I feel I won't be able to feel complete and happy until they are all paid and gone.

10. But I will feel a little better each time I pay some of it off.

11. At least it is turning around right now for me.

12. I know as I pay attention to how I feel it will be easier to draw more money in.

13. Maybe I have been focused on what I did not want and feeling bad about it.

14. I can see I had no option but to keep piling up debts while I felt so bad about them!

15. Maybe paying off my debts has actually nothing to do with how much money I earn.

16. I can see that the speed I can pay my debts off is connected with how I feel about it!

17. I have been doing it backwards!

18. I just need to keep working on my energy, my emotions and I know I will turn it around.
19. Soon I will form a new habit of feeling good about it.
20. I am feeling better already.
21. So what if I have debts? Everyone does! It doesn't need to define my self-esteem!
22. Wow, I am really getting the hang of this process!
23. I wonder what else I can use it on?
24. Maybe other things in my life make me feel bad and that is affecting my ability to pay off debts too!

Notice in all of these statements this person is not trying to find a way right now to fix the issue. They are simply true statements that feel a little bit better each time.

It is important to note that all we are doing in this process is shifting our vibrational frequency (or what feels true) a little each time we do this. Notice, if our person read the list of statements again the first one on the list would no longer feel true now. Conversely, before they applied the process the last statement on this list would have made them feel negative emotions as it would not have felt true.

If something negative was to manifest in their world, such as an unexpected bill that they couldn't pay, then they would probably go back to feeling bad about it until they applied the process again.

It is vital to note that once you apply the process you can never go back to where you were vibrationally before.

You may feel bad again when something shows up that you do not want but that is because you have a new level of attraction and you believe more than ever that you can get what you want.

Simply apply the process as many times as you need to for as long as you need to. Each time you do you, will find yourself in a different place to where you started. Even though nothing may have changed in the outer world as yet, you will be feeling better about it and therefore more able to allow it to come into physical form faster and easier.

Example 2. "I want a better relationship, my current partner doesn't treat me with respect and isn't romantic. I want to meet someone new who is nicer".

Now let's apply the same process to this desire and we will look for something that feels true but also feels a little better each time.

1. I want a better relationship, my current partner doesn't treat me with respect and isn't romantic. I want to meet someone new who is nicer.
2. Sometimes I do feel respected by my friends and that is nice.

3. Maybe I will meet someone soon that is nicer than my current partner.

4. In fact, the more I think about it the more likely it is to happen now that I know this process.

5. I can see I have been stuck noticing what I don't like about my girlfriend.

6. It feels better to even see why this has been happening.

7. I am starting to feel empowered by this process.

8. From now on I am going to pay much more attention to how I feel.

9. I can see that the way to meet a new girlfriend is simply to keep doing this!

10. Maybe I can work on myself a bit too, I am sure it's not all her fault that things aren't as good as they could be.

11. Actually, I can see I have not allowed her to act any differently as I had to keep manifesting the same things over and over.

Note that in statement 11 the person had thought this many times before but it always made him feel bad and disempowered because it did not feel true. Statement 11 would feel bad to him before now because he was not conscious of the process of manifestation. It made him blame and berate himself that he could not make it work.

We can begin to see how statements that were disempowering and made us feel worse, are now accessible and feel true as we apply this process. We cannot make too big a jump vibrationally all at once and so we start with tiny steps. As we progress and become very proficient at using this statement process, those steps can become bigger and bigger each time. For now all we are looking for is to feel just a little bit better.

Finally, for this lesson I shall leave you with the fact that when you apply the statement process to one desire, you are unknowingly applying it to everything you want. Why? Well because you are feeling better and so it is raising your vibrational point of attraction in all areas.

And really all any of us ever want is to feel good, and to keep feeling better and better. How we think we will get that is different for everyone but the basic thing that is wanted is happiness.

Exercises for Lesson Four

The exercises for this lesson are simply to try to apply the statement process to your desires from the previous lessons, or to anything you feel bad about right now.

Try and see how the process works and build your confidence in it.

CHAPTER 17

Conclusion

Each of these courses will change your life for the better. Studying them all in the order they are presented here has the power to put you beyond suffering once and for all. The tools and knowledge you have learnt here will help you for the rest of your life.

Some of these tools may not be easy to use at first and may take some work to get used to them. Each day is an opportunity to get better at using them.

It is normal that everyone will have some resistance to doing certain aspects of the courses and you may feel more challenged in some areas than others. I hold regular free Satsangs, where you can ask any questions or meet me online or in person. Help is available if you need it, please do reach out.

Please pass this book along and allow others you love to get the tools and resources to achieve a life of conscious creation and joy.

Namaste

Helen

APPENDIX

Summary of common names for the Noumenon

Below are some of the ways the Noumenon has been described in other teachings. For each set of terms there are two names. Reading through the list may help to awaken a recognition in you as you read and at certain times along the way different sets of terms may be more appealing than others.

They are all names for That Which Has No Name. Don't get attached to any name; look at what the name points to.

NOUMENON	PHENOMENA
Oneness	many
Allness	separation
Empty Mind	full mind
Unity	multiplicity
Silent Mind	noisy mind
Non-Duality	duality
"I" as Consciousness	"I" as a person
Nothingness	somethingness
Awakeness	sleep/dream

Consciousness	unconsciousness
Silence	sound
Subjectivity	object
Being	being someone/something
Stillness	movement
Presence	person
God	ego
Truth	falsehood
Formless	form
Reality	illusion
Knowingness	knowing about
Awareness	perception
Context	content
Infinite Field	finite being
Timeless	duration

If you would like more information about Helen, her live Satsangs, silent retreats and classes please contact us:

Visit our website at www.helenhamilton.org

Find us on facebook by searching @satsangwithhelenhamilton

Search for us on YouTube at satsangwithhelenhamilton

Email us at evolutionofspirit@gmail.com

Visit Helen's Author Page on Amazon:
https://www.amazon.com/-/e/B075X4DK7D

Printed and bound by CPI Group (UK) Ltd, Croydon, CR0 4YY